TOOLS FOR

THE DIRECT

ACCESS TRADER

Library of Congress Cataloging-in-Publication Data

Abell, Alicia
    Tools for the direct access trader : hardware, software, resources, and everything else
you need to get started / by Alicia Abell.
        p.   cm.
    ISBN 0-07-136248-7
    1. Electronic trading of securities—Handbooks, manuals, etc.   I. Title.

HG4515.95 .A235 2000
332.63'2'02854678—dc21

                                                                    00-065384

McGraw-Hill

A Division of The **McGraw·Hill** Companies

1 2 3 4 5 6 7 8 9 0   AGM/AGM   0 7 6 5 4 3 2 1

0-07-136248-7

The sponsoring editor for this book was Stephen Isaacs, the editing supervisor was Ruth W. Mannino,
and the production supervisor was Charles Annis.

Printed and bound by Quebecor/Martinsburg.

This publication is designed to provide accurate and authoritative information in regard to the subject
matter covered. It is sold with the understanding that neither the author nor the publisher is engaged
in rendering legal, accounting, or other professional service. If legal advice or other expert assistance
is required, the services of a competent professional person should be sought.
—*From a Declaration of Principles jointly adopted by a Committee of the American Bar Association
and a Committee of Publishers*

The viewpoints and content expressed by the author are her own and not those of Tradescape.com,
Inc. or any of its affiliated entities, employees, officers, directors, or authorized representatives (the
"Company"). The Company does not endorse any of the content contained herein and has not
verified the accuracy of any of the content. The information is not to be construed as investment
advice and any reliance on the content as contained herein is at the reader's sole risk and liability.

TradescapePro™ is a trademark of Tradescape.com, Inc.; NexTrade™, of NexTrade Holdings, Inc.;
Brut™, of The Brut ECN, LLC; and Ameritrade™, of Ameritrade, Inc. Island® is a registered trademark of The Island ECN, Inc. and E*TRADE® of E*TRADE, Inc. All other trademarked products
mentioned are used in an editorial fashion only, and to the benefit of the trademark owner, with no
intention of infringement of the trademark. Where such designations appear in this book, they have
been printed with initial caps.

This book is printed on recycled, acid-free paper containing a minimum of 50% recycled
de-inked fiber.

TOOLS FOR THE DIRECT ACCESS TRADER

Hardware, Software, Resources, and Everything Else You Need to Get Started

Alicia Abell

McGraw-Hill
New York   San Francisco   Washington, D.C.   Auckland   Bogotá
Caracas   Lisbon   London   Madrid   Mexico City   Milan
Montreal   New Delhi   San Juan   Singapore
Sydney   Tokyo   Toronto

To my family and friends for their support in this and all of my endeavors. I could not do it without you.

CONTENTS

PREFACE

Tools for the Direct Access Trader is part of the six-book series on direct access trading from McGraw-Hill. The series of books represents the first detailed look at every element of direct access trading for individuals interested in harnessing the amazing changes occurring in the world's financial markets. All the books contain a clear and basic approach to how to take advantage of direct access to the markets for your specific level of investing/trading. Direct access trading is for everyone, and in this series of books we show you how to take advantage of it if you only place a couple of trades a year, are starting to get more active in the markets, or even if you want to be a day trader. Take advantage of these revolutionary changes today, and start accessing the markets directly with direct access trading. Good luck!

TOOLS FOR
THE DIRECT
ACCESS TRADER

1

WHAT THIS BOOK
WILL DO FOR YOU

*The purpose of this book is to explain to all kinds of investors what
direct access trading tools are and how these tools can help them. Contrary to popular belief, direct access tools are not designed just for day
traders, although until now, day traders have been the ones who have
used them most. Direct access is actually targeted toward anyone who
trades frequently and is concerned about the details of his or her executions. Active online investors will find that direct access trading opens
up whole new worlds to them.*

This introduction will serve as a summary of the capabilities of direct
access and how to take advantage of them. Readers looking for more
information on a specific topic should refer to the chapter on that subject,
which will provide a more detailed explanation.

First, how does direct access trading differ from regular online investing? Well, when you place a trade order from your home or office computer, it is not usually placed directly into the market but is instead sent to a broker, frequently through an email type of system. The broker then places the order with a firm, which is not actually obligated to fill it until it is convenient for the firm to do so. This means that there is a period of time during which you can have an outstanding order that you are not able to cancel—and the market can move drastically before that order is actually executed.

Having an outstanding order for a few minutes, or even an hour, does not bother most people, especially those making long-term investments. However, if you plan on making quick, intraday trading decisions, this is a problem. You do not know if your order has been filled, and you cannot make other trading decisions based on that order until it has been confirmed. In addition, if you are placing larger orders of shares, where an eighth of a point can mean a couple of hundred extra dollars by not knowing the best price available, this can be substantial.

Thus, actually, there is very little difference between calling a broker and using an online broker. In both cases, you're still sending the order through an intermediary, and you still have to wait for this agent to procure the stock for you. Direct access trading, in contrast, lets you place your order directly.

Those who use direct access trading tools get information as fast as anyone else in the market—including brokers and institutional investors. Like them, direct access traders see exactly who wants to buy and sell stocks at all times and can react and execute in the same manner as these bigger players can.

This is so because direct access allows you to see something the general public does not: what is called the *inside market*, or the *level II market*. While level I information shows the best current buying and selling orders, level II access lets you see who is actually buying and selling individual stocks. It displays all the posted buyers and sellers of a stock, identifying them and specifying at what price and how many shares they are willing to trade. As prices rise and fall, bids and asks are cleared, and then higher or lower prices are shown. Real-time reports then confirm the trades, their price, and their size.

This means you can see big institutional investors like Goldman Sachs or Merrill Lynch or Morgan Stanley lining up to buy or sell a certain stock and then see confirmation when their trade is executed. Level II information is very important for day traders and very active online investors because it allows them to see what is happening beneath the surface of the market. Without it, you could miss changes in the market. Level II helps you to get a clearer picture of a stock, focus in on relevant data better, and execute orders faster. It is the main tool that bridges the gap that existed between individual investors and professional traders for so many years.

Most direct access trading tools are derived from software that was developed originally for professional traders and has been modified for use by varying levels of investors. Trading firms recognize that different people need different options. Because they know that the success of their software in the marketplace is tied to how many different investors they can reach, they make a major effort to provide a variety of choices.

However, the direct access tools used by day traders and those used by average investors are not all that different. In fact, the fundamental information being accessed is extremely similar. It is how that information is used that distinguishes the two: The day trader uses it to make split-second decisions between buying and selling that the average investor simply does not need to make.

The average investor is usually focused on particular areas of the market that he or she is particularly knowledgeable about, whereas the day trader reacts to market movements based solely on the movements themselves in an effort to make short-term profits.

Despite this distinction, there is one advantage that real-time direct access provides to everyone, from the average investor to the active day trader: lower costs. Those who use direct access are able to execute their own orders at costs that are lower than what brokers are quoting for the market and can avoid giving an intermediary a cut of the action.

Not surprisingly, direct access trading tools are putting pressure on more traditional online brokers. Many people believe that if these brokers do not adapt to the new technology and offer direct access trading, they will lose the customers who provide the most transactional volume.

Even among direct access firms, there is competition to see which can best adapt for the future. The key to winning this battle will be the ability to offer investors all the liquidity in a stock in one area. Trading systems will need to have access to all the electronic communication networks (ECNs) out there (see Chapter 4) through one single interface; otherwise, they will not be offering enough liquidity.

Right now, direct access trading tools are used mainly to trade on the Nasdaq (National Association of Securities Dealers Automated Quotation

System) exchange. There is some movement toward trading this way on the New York Stock Exchange (NYSE), but it is not yet common. However, the pressure that direct access has put on the NYSE (people have witnessed the value of an electronic model) should cause some of its stocks—perhaps 100 or so particularly active ones—to begin trading on electronic exchanges sometime soon.

Furthermore, many people believe that we are moving toward one single global market and that, eventually, direct access tools will allow people to invest in all kinds of exchanges, including foreign ones and the bonds and options markets. This means that we should see more and more exchanges converting to an electronic model. Ultimately, we are likely to have a 24-hour-a-day, 7-days-a-week global electronic market.

How will this affect average investors? First, they will have more choices. They will be able to choose to have direct access applications, information, and technology for very little cost. Second, the back end (the part you do not see, the part that makes everything you want to see show up on your computer screen) of almost any trading technology will be far superior to the way it is today.

In the meantime, it is important to look for direct access trading software that is both sophisticated and user-friendly. Look for a package that is inexpensive, fast, and reliable and provides all the different functionality you think you might need. As for a computer to run the software on, unless you are a professional trader, you should not require more than an up-to-date piece of machinery with at least 128 megabytes of RAM.

You also will need a high-speed modem and one or more Internet service providers (ISPs) to connect you to the Internet. Different ISPs have different traffic patterns, and certain of them can be difficult to connect to depending on the time of day. Having access to a number of different ISPs (which should have different traffic patterns) can help eliminate this annoyance.

What about tools other than level II data? What kinds of bells and whistles should you look for? This will be discussed in more detail in Chapter 4, but in a nutshell, pick the secondary tools that best meet your style. The most important thing is to find a software package that is a good combination of everything you feel you need to be an informed trader.

Any direct access trading package, however—no matter what its bells and whistles and no matter which firm offers it—needs to meet certain standards. Keep these in mind when choosing your direct access firm.

First is speed, the main factor affecting the quality of your information and the success of your trades. Both the speed of your quotes (your level II information) and the speed of executions need to be top-notch. Direct access trading deals in milliseconds, and your system needs to be up to the task.

Another important quality to look for is the functionality and appearance of the front end (what you actually see on your computer screen). This is so because the front end is your window to the market; it is what gives you the ability to process all the information you need to make good trading decisions. The front end is where all this information is organized, and it should be presented in a clear, easy-to-understand fashion that you can react to. Many trading systems look very similar, so you must research what the differences in systems are.

Look at the information on the screen. Is it easy to understand or confusing? Is everything that you need right there and easy to see? Does superfluous information get in the way? Even a very well organized screen can be overwhelming with information.

Find software that does an exceptional job of filtering data and only shows you information that is pertinent to you. The trading screen should be simplified and streamlined. It should feature position management and level II quote information and include stock-picking filters and other tools that give you the ability to filter out stocks based on a number of different factors.

Two other factors to consider when choosing a direct access system are connectivity and reliability. The option that gives you a single window to the greatest amount of liquidity should be a serious contender. This is so because the only way to benefit from all the liquidity pools that are out there is through a consolidated portal to the market. Your system should be impeccably reliable as well. The challenge is to find a package that balances reliability and speed, since too much emphasis on one can compromise the other.

One last quality to consider when picking a direct access firm is its reputation. Direct access trading is very new, so even the oldest firms have only been around for a few years. Just do not pick a company that is just starting out or whose whole business is not devoted to direct access trading.

Today, the direct access industry is highly fragmented. There are countless different technologies and trading platforms. However, this is the way most technology and other business improvements start out: The industry starts off extremely fragmented, and then companies begin to merge and consolidate. Standards emerge, and there is a race to the finish.

The key to winning that race will be figuring out what different levels of connectivity and what levels of intelligence as to how an order is routed customers want. Firms will compete to be the end-to-end solution provider for all kinds of companies and individuals.

Right now, most firms offer only level II quote products geared toward traders who need or use this information to make trading decisions. Even though it is not hard to learn to understand these quotes, there is no question that they are geared to sophisticated, very active traders. Therefore, in order to reach more of a mass audience, these firms are working on new level I products, scheduled to appear on the market shortly. These products will be geared toward users who want real-time data and want to benefit from the latest technology but do not need full level II quotes to make split-second trading decisions.

However, even level I traders will need to have a good grasp of how the market works, as well as understand some basic direct access trading terms. Chapter 4 addresses this topic fully. Then it discusses the differences between the New York Stock Exchange and the Nasdaq. The NYSE is an auction-oriented market, which means that its prices are determined by competitive bidding between traders who represent buyers and sellers. Conversely, the Nasdaq is a negotiated market, in which transactions occur over a computer network consisting of numerous trading terminals instead of a physical trading floor.

On the NYSE and other auction markets, someone called a *specialist* is in charge of the transactions in each stock. Every transaction of that stock has to go through the specialist. The specialist acts as an auctioneer and matches various buy and sell orders More than one stock can be assigned to each specialist, but there can be no more than one specialist assigned to each stock.

Specialists must make sure the market in the stocks they cover is fair and organized at all times. They also must make sure that there is a constant availability of buyers and sellers. This means that if someone wants to buy or sell a stock and there is no one else to take the other end of the transaction, the specialist must do so from his or her own account. This guarantees that there is always stability and liquidity in the stock—even when there are no buyers and sellers in the public market. In return for ensuring that there is always liquidity in a stock, specialists are allowed to charge a markup on the stocks they cover and to profit from the difference between the buying and selling prices, known as the *spread.*

On the Nasdaq, in contrast, orders are not routed through a single entity like a specialist but instead are posted as bids and offers on an electronic network. As on the NYSE, however, there are entities that facilitate and profit from the transactions on these exchanges. These are called *market makers.* Like specialists, market makers are intermediaries in buying and selling. But unlike on the NYSE, more than one market maker can represent each stock.

To ensure that customers will always be able to trade in a stock, market makers must always have a price at which they will buy and sell the stocks they represent. As with specialists, they get to profit from the spread on trades in return for this responsibility. Market makers will always sell you a stock at a price that is fractionally higher than the one they will buy it from you at. This is legal for both market makers and specialists because it is considered a fair tradeoff; because they risk their own capital to maintain an orderly market and act as both buyers and sellers when required, these entities are allowed to make money from the spread.

Chapter 4 also explains the Small Order Execution System (SOES), which is the automated system that lets you bypass brokers and place orders of up to 1000 shares of a Nasdaq stock. SOES is what ensures the routing and execution of your order by the market maker offering the best price. The SOES assures small traders that their orders will be filled and also assures day traders that their orders will be filled instantaneously.

SOES was created in the wake of the 1987 stock market crash in order to make sure that both market makers and individual investors could get their orders filled during a high-volume or low-liquidity market. Until 1987, there was no such system, and market makers simply did not have to fill orders when it was not convenient for them. This obviously put small investors at a great disadvantage. Not surprisingly, then, small investors immediately took advantage of SOES, with something called *SOES trading.* This involved watching the market closely and entering and leaving it extremely quickly for fast, short-term gains—what is now known as *day trading.*

Electronic communication networks (ECNs) are another important tool for direct access traders. ECNs you may have heard of include

SelectNet, Instinet, Island, and Archipelago. Each of these is a network that allows individual traders and institutions to post, buy, and sell orders directly to the Nasdaq. ECNs are the main means to trade more shares than those allowed on SOES. Unlike on SOES, which shows the identity of those posting bids and offers (as well as their order size), bids and offers on ECNs are absorbed into a larger amount to reflect the total sum of everyone using the ECN to trade. As a result, the number of shares posted to trade on an ECN is more a reflection of actual interest in a stock than are individual asks on SOES.

ECNs are networks of traders, not firms that represent stocks, so they are not responsible for ensuring liquidity or taking the opposite side of any trade, like specialists and market makers. While ECNs are often more reliable and flexible than SOES (shorting stocks is much easier through ECNs, for example), they also can be risky. This is so because there is no guarantee that someone will buy or sell at your posted price on an ECN (SOES, in contrast, guarantees that you will be able to exit a stock).

Right now, all the ECNs stand alone, but recently, there has been talk of connecting them, a development that would greatly increase liquidity for all market participants.

A level II trading screen allows you to see on which ECNs various bids and asks have been posted. It also sorts the bids and asks according to price and the order in which they were received. Market makers are represented by four-letter symbols.

After figuring out what all the different direct access terms and tools mean and allow you to do, you then have to learn how to profit from them. Chapter 6 explains some of the different indicators traders use to gauge the general sentiment and likely direction of the market and to predict the price movements of individual stocks.

The overall health of the U.S. economy is, of course, important, as are various social and political events. Then there is the law of supply and demand, which determines which way the market will trend. Its direction is a clear result of the volume of buyers versus sellers.

For long-term investors, short-term fluctuations in price are not very significant. For very active traders, however, moment-to-moment supply and demand are much more important. This is why traders use what are known as *market sentiment indicators* to help them understand the market on a day-to-day basis. Chapter 6 explains some of these sentiment indicators, including public/specialist short sales data, the Chicago Board of Exchange put/call ratio, and the advance/decline line.

It also covers technical indicators, which are the result of studying various patterns and relationships in a stock's behavior. Technical analysis is most often contrasted with fundamental analysis, which aims to find the true value of a company instead of looking for clues to short-term price movements. Some of the technical indicators discussed include moving averages, support and resistance, breakouts and breakdowns, and overbought/oversold indicators. Daily, weekly, and seasonal patterns such as momentum patterns, best percentage days, the Friday-to-Monday pattern, and the end-of-quarter bias are also noted.

In the end, however, the main differences between professionals and beginners are experience and education. You can have all the tools, understand the lingo, and be familiar with all sorts of indicators. You can spend thousands of dollars trying to learn about trading. But if you have not practiced doing it with real money, you will not master it.

This book cannot do much for you in the way of experience, but it can help you with education. You need to read as much as you can about the stock market, although you do need to have filters to weed out the nonsense. Besides reading this and other primers on direct access trading, you will want to watch news sources like CNBC, Bloomberg TV, and CNN. You will want to read print publications such as *Investors Business Daily,* the *Wall Street Journal, Barron's,* and *Business Week.* You will want to consult market sentiment polling services to find out about extremes of optimism or pessimism and keep up with various newswires and Web sites.

Then, of course, the next step is to just get started. Make sure you have a steady cash flow at first; otherwise, bills will eat up your money, and you will feel pressure each month to make money to pay them (not a good feeling for a beginner). Try to emulate the characteristics of successful traders—knowledge, confidence, an open mind, and self-discipline—and you will be on your way.

Good luck!

2

DIRECT ACCESS
TRADING TOOLS

The first question many people ask when they hear about direct access trading tools is whether or not these tools are designed for them. Are they really just for day traders, or are they something that can be used by everyone? The answer is simple: Direct access is designed for very active online investors, day traders, and everyone in between. Active online investors appreciate the freedom and control over their trades that direct access gives them, and day traders can use the tools either as a supplement to their professional system or as their main trading system itself. In the end, direct access trading tools are best for people who trade a lot or for investors who are concerned about the details of their executions and worry about getting the best execution possible.

Many people lambaste direct access trading (especially day trading), and there are certainly risks involved. These make it all the more important for people to understand exactly what they are doing. The purpose of this book is to show the good side of the new technologies—how they are being used and what they can mean for the individual investor.

"It's wonderful, because people don't have to rely on other people," says one trader. "They don't have to rely on the sort of old school stuffed shirt mentality that I [the stockbroker] will control the stock. . . . I think that's wonderful. It's pure empowerment. It's really a microcosm of what the Internet is all about. You can go get things yourself." Thus, if you are interested in controlling your own financial destiny and you are interested in empowerment, keep reading.

Before you decide whether direct access trading is for you, it is important to understand how it differs from online investing. The distinction is simple: When a traditional online investor places an order from a home computer, the order is not usually placed directly into the market. Instead, it is sent to a broker. The broker can then do a number of things with that order. The broker can go out and post his or her own bid or offer on the market (which, as an electronic trader, you can see from home). Or the broker can sell the order to a big-name market maker who will go out and get the stock for him or her. This means that the market maker, the one the broker sold the order to, is buying the order flow and the volume on the stock. Or finally, the broker can trade against the order. This means that rather than place his or her own bid in your name, the broker can go out and buy the stock at a cheaper price and sell it to you at the price you want and make money on the differential.

The technologies used for online investing and direct access trading are different as well. Online investing uses an email-type system to actually route orders. This has certainly brought convenience to the user and is a good adaptation of the Internet in that it allows individuals to manage their investments over the Web. But it involves no innovation in execution ability; email simply replaces the telephone as a means to place orders.

When you use a Charles Schwab, or a TD Waterhouse, or an Ameritrade, what happens is that an email is sent to one of the firm's brokers or to its system at large. Most of these systems were built in the early 1980s. The systems look at the order, process it, and check whether or not it is marginable. If so, it might be sent out to a market-making firm.

Once the order is out there, you usually cannot cancel it. This is so because the order has actually left the brokerage and is now in the hands of the market maker. If you have placed a market order, for example, most brokerages require you to cancel it before the market opens at 9:30 A.M. It also can take a long time for a market order you are depending on to get filled. This is so because market makers have the ability to turn their autoexecution function off, and this usually happens in the most critical times in the day—from 9:30 to 10:00 A.M. and from 3:30 to 4:00 P.M.—or whenever the market is moving very fast.

Therefore, a firm that gets your market order is not really obligated to fill it until it is convenient for the firm to do so. There is a period of time during which you can have a market order that is outstanding that you are not able to cancel—and the market can move pretty dramatically before that order actually gets executed.

The systems are not designed for rapid order confirmation, and you usually get confirmation by email. Sometimes it takes a while to update the database. The nature of the technology is so slow that you do not see confirmations in real time.

Consequently, with an online brokerage firm, some people have orders that are live for 15 minutes—even an hour—and they are unable to get confirmation of their trades. This does not bother some people, but it is like trading a little bit blindly. You do not know if your order is live. You do not know if it is confirmed. You cannot make other trading decisions based on confirmations you do not have. Ten minutes is too long to have to wait to make intraday trading decisions.

Thus there is very little difference between calling a broker as you did 10 years ago and using an online broker today. In both cases, you are still sending the order through a broker, and you still have to wait for that broker to make a move for you in your name to get that stock. You still have to wait to get confirmation through the broker.

Direct access trading, in contrast, uses connectivity to the electronic markets like Nasdaq to actually route orders directly instead of via email or via brokers. This gives the user the ability to actually see the information electronically in a real-time, dynamic environment. The user gets information as fast as anyone else—including brokers, market makers, and institutional investors—in the market. Therefore, when perceiving any changes in that information, the user can react and execute in the same manner as other market participants can.

Unlike traditional investors, direct access traders can put in their own bids if they want to buy a stock. Or they can go after a market maker and buy the stock from SOES or an electronic communication network (ECN, to be discussed in Chapter 4). Direct access traders literally can buy and sell a stock 100 times before the traditional online investor can get confirmation of a trade. It is a different world because you do not have to rely on anybody.

There is also a difference between the information direct access traders and traditional investors see. Direct access traders see everything the broker who places orders for the online trader does. They see all the quotes—all the market makers bidding, all the market makers offering. The software grabs all the pertinent information, focuses it, and directs it to the trader. This information indicates which price market makers want to buy at and which they want to sell at. Electronic traders see all the sales that occur in Nasdaq in a particular stock in real time.

The only thing that electronic traders do not see that brokers might is volume on a stock that a broker may be privy to because his or her company has a deal with a certain company. However, as far as who is bidding and who is offering, electronic traders see it all. In many cases, electronic traders see more than brokers because of the full connectivity to ECNs, which is not high on the priority list of many brokers. "Their game is relationships, and their game is executing the orders," a representative of a direct access trading firm explains. "Our game is helping you execute the best order, and our relationships have nothing to do with it."

Therefore, as you can see, direct access trading does not simply capitalize on one of the primary benefits of the Internet: convenience. It moves beyond convenience and furthers the uses of the Web by giving investors the ability to actually benefit from real-time information and real-time execution capacities.

Prior to direct access trading, it was impossible for the average individual to execute an order in a truly time-sensitive or informed way. This was so because trading decisions were based on information that was no longer timely or no longer relevant. And there was no direct access to execution venues. Direct access trading, in contrast, gives the average individual the ability to trade in and benefit from the markets electronically. This is an example of technology being used in a truly innovative way.

The idea behind direct access trading tools is to give individuals the broadest range of execution possible or, as a developer at one electronic trading firm says, "getting them in contact with the most liquidity in the fastest possible way." Trading firms recognize that people are different and need options. They know that the ability of their software to reach different people and its ability to grow in the marketplace are tied closely to how many different ways it gives for people to buy and sell stocks. Ten different people might each need a different option for getting out of a stock, and an experienced trader might need all ten (which one is used depending on the particular situation). This ability to get out of a stock in many different ways satisfies both the great trader and less experienced investors.

To this end, electronic trading firms are continually developing better and better software tools to give them an advantage over other firms (this healthy competition works in the customer's favor, of course). Most of the development has to do with integration of aspects of the back end— the parts you do not see, like servers, execution platforms, and the mechanisms of information delivery. All of this comes out to one front-end piece, i.e., your computer screen, which provides easily accessible information that flows correctly according to how your eye moves and is driven by speed.

The back end of direct access trading systems is incredibly complicated, and it is a Herculean task to coordinate all the different pieces to make the data look user-friendly on the front end. It has taken years to learn how to manage the millions of pieces of information and bring them onto one simple front-end interface. Many trading systems used in the past acted as a sort of a beta test. Trading firms developing software now have learned from their mistakes and know how to streamline much of the coding on the back end to make the online product faster. Most direct access trading software comes from tools that were actually developed for the firms' professional systems and modified to make an online product.

Because the user interfaces are quite simple, learning to use these tools is relatively easy, although learning to manage the amount of information offered to you can be another matter. In general, there are four levels of development. The first is learning how to read the screen, to understand how the information is coming at you. The second is learning how to read and process. The third is learning how to read, process, *and* react. The fourth is learning how to read, process, and react *manually.* In other words, your brain can be ready to act, but can your hands do it? Each stage takes a lot of work.

Along the way, you learn to develop and follow calculated strategies, which requires strict discipline. Things do not always make sense. There are certain rules you can follow, but a lot of the rules you have to develop yourself, through your experience. You must learn to follow these rules—but also to recognize the exceptions to these rules and know when to break them. "It's not gambling by any means," says one trader. "You can't make the kind of money these guys are making with gambling. But you need to develop your own strategy of risk to reward."

There are a couple of keys to mastering these four stages of using direct access tools. One, obviously, is patience. Another is acclimation. You need to acclimate your eyes to what is happening on the screen—to get your mind used to understanding the information. The ability to process fractions is also important. Then there is the physical aspect. You need to be able to move your hands extremely quickly. "It's a race out there," says one trader. "It really is."

The direct access tools used by extremely active traders and those used by average investors differ only in scope. The fundamental information being accessed is very similar. The sophisticated investor who is just starting level II quote trading has at his or her fingertips the same fundamental information that is available to the very active trader. But the use of level II quotes empowers the active trader to make split-second decisions between buying and selling that the investor probably does not need—or want—to make. The main distinction is that the active day trader has a greater need and ability to process more and different types of information than the average investor.

An active day trader, for example, will have multiple level II quote boxes open, will display a larger position manager showing a greater number of stocks that he or she is following, and will have different Nasdaq filters showing a larger amount of and more sensitive streaming information than the average investor. The average investor is more focused on certain segments and areas of the market that he or she is particularly educated about, whereas the day trader reacts intuitively to market movements based solely on the movements themselves, for movement's sake. The day trader needs all kinds of filters in order to follow all the Nasdaq or even the entire electronic market. The day trader looks for opportunity anywhere, and such opportunities can arise at any moment. The online investor does not need the same scope of functionality.

As a result, the average investor may not need as much bandwidth or modem speed as a day trader. Data provided to the trader are relatively large and do not always fit a 56-K modem.

Once again, the software developers from direct access trading firms realize all this and design software accordingly. "There's an intimidation factor involved . . . ," says one trader. "If you . . . put the same tools that the day trader uses and sees every single day in front of . . . [average investors], they're never going to access it; they're not going to gain anything out of it. What you need to do is really get the most important, critical information that's necessary to make the decisions and that provides them with the same functionality from the information perspective—or similar functionality from an information perspective. You have to find what that is, refine it, and kind of repackage it for the online investor. In some ways, it's a resale market."

In other words, there is a direct access tool for everyone. Despite the differences, there is one advantage that real-time direct access provides to everyone, from the average investor to the active day trader, and this is the ability to eliminate inefficiency costs. The user is able to directly access the markets, and instead of giving a "middleman" a cut—known as the *spread*—traders are actually able to execute their own orders at costs that are lower than what brokers are quoting for the market. Without middle management, users can tighten and even eliminate spreads for the first time.

Because this actual cost includes more than commission—it also encompasses what you lose because of the inefficiency of a trade—these savings can be quite significant. One trader explains it this way: "If somebody's trading over an E*TRADE or Datek or a Schwab . . . or any of those . . . [online brokerage firms] where they send an order in to buy a stock and the worst market order is sent to one of those systems—what they're essentially doing is saying, 'Fine, I'm willing to pay the $10 or $20, the cost in commission. I think that's pretty cheap.' But what they're really doing is saying, 'I'm willing to, say, buy 100 shares of stock in Microsoft for $52.' But if they could have bought that stock at 51¾, that's $250 [saved]. That's the real cost of execution. . . . The fact is that in some ways they're paying three times—this is the whole analogy."

Not surprisingly, direct access trading tools are going to—and have already started to—put a lot of pressure on the established online brokers. Many people believe that if these brokers do not adapt to the new technology and update their systems, they are going to lose their most valuable customers—the ones who provide the most transactional volume.

Here's how one trader explains it: "Ninety-nine percent of the time, the consumer wins out. The demands of the consumer, the education of the consumer, force companies to adapt. The ones who turn a blind eye and kind of turn their back on what's happening in the direct access markets, and what's happening with education of the consumer, are the ones that are going to be the first to be left behind. And those that adapt the fastest, those that are able to see what's happening in the market and see what's happening with the electronic direct access trading, are the quickest to integrate the systems into their own—to adapt to it, to learn. . . . And not just with front ends, but with actual fundamental changes to how orders are routed in the back end, and the structures which have kept the online trading, online investing, going. Unless [online brokerage firms] are able to fundamentally change those, they're going to be left behind."

Currently, many online brokerage firms are partnering with and taking equity stakes in electronic communication networks (ECNs). Perhaps they are hoping that if they invest in these ECNs, they will be able to route their trades through them.

However, many people believe that we are moving toward one single global market and that brokerage firms will need to be able to feed off of trades on all the ECNs, not just one. In this scenario, the ECNs will be liquidity centers. In and of themselves, they are not greatly efficient, but as a combined entity—when they are consolidated through a portal mechanism—they will be extremely valuable. The key to the future is the ability to gain all the liquidity in a stock in one area. Trading systems will need to have access to all the ECNs through one single interface simply because otherwise they will be missing out on access to an enormous amount of market liquidity.

Eventually, direct access tools will allow people to invest in all kinds of exchanges, including foreign ones. As one software developer says, "The question isn't what a leading company like Tradescape or any other active trading firm can do. The question is right now, 'Can the exchanges keep up with our needs?' "

Right now, direct access trading tools are used primarily to trade on the Nasdaq. There is some movement toward trading on the New York Stock Exchange (NYSE), but it is not really possible yet. There is no real competitive advantage that anyone can offer because there is no source of electronic liquidity. To trade with direct access, you need to be able to execute an electronic order that is all but guaranteed.

However, the pressure of ECNs on the NYSE should cause some stocks—perhaps 100 or so active ones—to begin trading on electronic exchanges sometime soon. "I think NYSE's smart enough and is going to get involved in that and make sure that they themselves are the ones behind it as opposed to being the ones behind the curve," says one trader.

Most people see this as the next major trend in the electronic market game: more and more exchanges converting to an electronic model. Direct connectivity ultimately will apply to international exchanges as well, and the trend toward a 24-hour-a-day, 7-days-a-week global electronic market is already apparent. Many traders believe that soon the different electronic markets are going to link up by using the same technology standards, which will allow for the trading of securities anywhere worldwide, at any time. Certain stocks will become the global stocks, the global companies (and will have a subset of symbols to identify them as such). Some of the newer markets that are developing—in the Far East and Europe, for example—may even adapt to the new technology standards right off the bat, or will at least look to partner with companies that can offer these technological capabilities.

It might be only 50 to 100 of the top stocks on each of the different global exchanges at first, but many people believe that it will happen. There will be mergers and partnerships between the Nasdaq and various exchanges around the world. The relative success of Nasdaq and the value that has been gotten out of it through electronic trading will propel the other markets, including the bond market and the options market.

More philosophically put, the growth of connectivity in general means that direct access to the markets will soon spread over into other areas. The natural evolution of technology will result in the natural evolution of how people need to be able to trade. There is so much power in direct access technology and so much power in the interaction of individuals with the markets through that technology that it has an almost gravitational pull. Any movement forward pushes people toward a certain standard, which means that those who are not meeting that standard feel left behind. And feeling left behind pushes people—and organizations— to move forward so that they can compete economically. Thus direct access will be available for much more than just stocks on the Nasdaq.

One trader explains it this way: "If there's any type of fragmented liquidity—which is the case in 99 percent of most markets out there— there's a use for this technology. . . . Anything from lumber to bonds to fixed income. . . ."

How are all these developments going to affect the average investor in the future? In a couple of ways. First, investors will have a choice. They will be able to choose whether they want to have new front ends—

which include some of the direct access applications, information, and technology—or stick with the old kind. Second, all investors will be affected on the back end. Order flow structures are going to evolve into a much freer environment where Schwab or E*TRADE customers will be connected to superior back ends. And if Schwab and E*TRADE do not adapt to provide superior back ends, then a new generation of online brokers will arise to offer the front convenience of a Schwab combined with the back-end execution ability of direct access firms.

"So it's really going to be the evolution of choice—the liberalization of choice in some ways—where users are going to have the ability to say, 'You know what, I don't even want to use the simple HTML interface that I've currently been using on Schwab, but I want to have access to the superior execution ability at lower transaction costs,' " explains one trader. "That's the choice they're going to have. The best benefit of technology is not something which is forced upon people, but the availability of choice and the . . . freedom to kind of move in a more efficient manner."

The future also promises greater ubiquity, as the technology behind direct access trading spreads to the average investor. Says one trader at a direct access firm, "What E*TRADE did with the ATMs, they bought ATMs. We're going to be able to basically sell a stock if you need cash. I don't know if you're aware of that. It's a pretty indicative move of where things may be going."

Finally, the future of direct access holds exciting developments like portable trading systems, voice activation, and handheld devices. Handhelds, for example, will almost certainly be used to do some direct access trading. People will have the ability to monitor their portfolios and current positions on the fly. One trader calls it a "purification" of the product to the point where "it fits within the data, the bandwidth, and the screen available." It is the evolution from "the day trading shop to the online trader sitting at his [or her] computer at home to the Palm Pilot."

It will allow you to avoid spending hours on the phone trying to reach your broker and instead let you place a trade directly through your Palm Pilot. Can you imagine what the next use of direct access technology will be?

Direct access traders see something the general public does not: the inside market, or the level II market. The level II market includes information that helps traders develop and confirm their trading strategies. For example, a direct access trader can see market makers like Goldman

Sachs or Merrill Lynch or Morgan Stanley lining up to buy or sell a certain stock. These are the actions that often determine a stock's movement. Direct access traders see the impetus for movement as well as support and resistance at certain levels in a stock

In other words, if a stock is going up and it passes through a price level of \$40½, a direct access trader can see when Goldman Sachs comes in to sell the stock at \$40¾, positioning itself at what it sees as the end of a movement by preparing to sell. Or the trader might see Goldman Sachs buying a certain stock all day long. People trading from home can use this action of a Goldman Sachs or another market maker—consistently selling to a huge institution that is just buying and buying, not lowering the price at which it wants to buy, and accepting basically all orders.

Along with seeing who's buying and selling individual stocks on a superficial level, direct access traders receive lots of information on their computer screens through something called the *contraprints* or the *contrabroker*. The *contraprints* tell you when a trade is confirmed, when a trade is executed across an ECN like SelectNet or Island or Instinet. They tell you whom you bought from or sold to. This is important information because it tells you if one of the large market makers bought or sold stock from you, which tends to identify the trend of the stock or the value of its relative strength for the day. In fact, many people react solely to the contraprints. (And if you can beat those people to receiving the information, then you will be ahead of the curve—and ahead in your ability to profit.)

SUMMARY

Direct access trading tools for individuals are a relatively new phenomenon; however, Wall Street professionals have been using comparable tools since the inception of trading. When trading first started, as the number of individuals trading and the number of securities traded continued to grow by leaps and bounds, it led to the rise of numerous "middlemen" who profited greatly by bridging the gap between buyers and sellers. In addition, the tools needed to monitor the real-time activities of the stock market were extremely expensive and could be afforded only by brokerage firms. Only recently, with the creation of SOES (Small Order Execution System), ECNs, new regulations allowing direct access, and the proliferation of the Internet are individuals finally being able to access the markets directly. Most notably, the Internet has been a very powerful weapon in helping the individual trader gain access to information, even in real time. Resources such as level II quotes, a must for every direct access trader, could never have been available to individuals if it were not for the Internet. In addition, the way data are presented to a trader is now done in a much more user-friendly fashion. Instead of just blips and random numbers floating around on a screen, direct access trading firms have taken it on themselves to create interfaces that can be understood by all at any level. Direct access is now here to stay, and the tools used to access the markets directly are getting easier to use every day. In some ways it is even easier than investing online through a normal broker; however, direct access trading tools are much more powerful and therefore require a much greater understanding before they are used.

Direct access trading tools are quite similar to the tools you would use to invest online. The difference, however, is that you are using them in a completely different way. Because direct access trading can be Web-based, just the same as online investing, the major differences are happening behind the scenes. Your direct access trading firm deals with them and then creates an easy-to-use interface for you to harness the power of such things previously only available to professional traders on Wall Street. These "things" mostly encompass the way your trades are routed, such as through ECNs. By doing your homework on direct access trading firms (brief descriptions are included later in this book) and by talking to other direct access traders, you will be able to get a good idea of which firm provides the direct access trading tools that best suit your needs. There are a number of direct access trading firms, which means that you can align your trading profile and technology comfort level with the one that best suits your needs.

Direct access trading is the way of the future. Individuals who spend the time to get comfortable with the tools now will be able to capitalize on new opportunities as they arise much more quickly than other individuals. Who would not have wished they could have learned how to use direct access trading tools to get in on some of the extremely hot Internet initial public offerings (IPOs) that skyrocketed through the roof on their first day of trading? While online investors sat back and prayed they could get shares, even offering market price and hoping not to pay too much, direct access traders simply went directly into the market and found a seller and bought them. Although we are simplifying the process somewhat, those early adopters who understand how to use direct access trading tools and the right situations to use the tools based on their trading profile were able to capitalize on opportunities such as these. However, we are in stage one of what direct access trading will enable individuals to do. Today, it is to predominantly trade Nasdaq stocks. In the very near future it will be stocks on the NYSE. And then what's next? Bonds, pork bellies, lumber, anything you can think of. And in no time you will be able to do it from your computer, a personal digital assistant (PDA), or even your cellular phone. Direct access trading tools are the way of the future for all individuals—most people just do not realize it yet.

So how do you capitalize on the great direct access trading tools? It takes time. Like anything else, you need to invest a lot of time and a bit of money to really get going. It is also extremely important to identify very specifically how you plan on using direct access trading tools. Direct access trading tools are very powerful, and it is extremely important to stick to your goals and not become overwhelmed with what they enable you to do. One of the main reasons that regulations existed for so long to prevent individuals from having direct access was the fear that they would use the tools improperly. However, with the advent of online investing, the Internet, and the growing frustration by individuals locked out of Wall Street, the markets eventually capitulated. So as we move on to what types of direct access trading tools you need to access the markets, keep in mind that it takes time to learn how to use these tools and, more important, to determine how you want to use them. Anyone can learn, regardless of their previous experience with stocks or investing, but it takes time and a dedication to learn.

QUESTIONS TO ASK YOURSELF

1 How are these tools different from what I have been using in the past?

2 What is my experience level with the markets in general?

3 How comfortable am I with online trading?

4 How comfortable am I with the Internet and computers in general?

5 How comfortable am I with the fast-paced nature of direct access trading?

6 What type of direct access trader do I plan on being?

7 What types of direct access trading tools am I not yet comfortable with?

8 What do I not understand about direct access trading tools?

9 What do I need to learn more about?

10 Whom can I talk to to learn more about direct access trading tools?

3

WHAT DO I NEED?

If you decide to make the move from active online investing to direct access trading, you will need certain tools. What are these tools? How are they different from what is used by standard online investors?

In most cases, you need pretty simple hardware and software for direct access trading. The most important thing is to find trading software, also called an *execution system,* with superior back-end routing technology and front-end innovation. In other words, you need software that combines sophisticated access with user-friendliness and convenience. Make sure you choose a platform that is fast, cheap, reliable, and provides all the liquidity and functionality you will need. The backbone behind your software determines the strength of your network.

Unless you have traded in an office before—traded for a living (in which case you will want a very up-to-date computer)—you do not need a supercomputer to run trading software, just a good piece of desktop machinery. If you are using an Intel-based system, you will need the latest Pentium processor—a Pentium III processor, probably a 400 or higher.

It is also a good idea to have at least 128 megabytes of RAM, and a fixed-gigabyte hard drive will give you open available space to grow as well. Although some systems require a 21-inch monitor, 17-inch monitors are more than adequate.

Next, you will need a high-speed modem—the higher the better, although a 56-K modem is adequate—and one or more Internet service providers (ISPs) to connect you to the Internet. If you can open up America Online (AOL), you can run most trading platforms. However, if you can get digital service line (DSL) service or a connection to a T1 line, you will be even that much better off.

"You just need an Internet connection. Any Internet connection," says one direct access software developer. "A nice jug of water, pen and paper, and you're ready to go. It [the software] is geared toward not making you do any work, other than being able to log onto the system and concentrating real hard. It's made to have you not worry about any of those things. That's the entire reason for it." However, there is no denying that having a faster connection to the Internet is definitely a plus. Many of the larger phone networks such as Verizon, AT&T, and RCN are offering DSL packages that can run anywhere from $60 to $100 a month.

If you are trading from home and your connection uses a streaming, real-time, dynamic trading platform—whether it is a Java applet or another application—you probably should have multiple ISPs. (It is not necessary to have a DSL or broadband connection.) This is so because different ISPs have different traffic patterns, and depending on the time of day, certain of them are almost impossible to connect to. It is very hard to get good bandwidth through ISPs. They have queues that build up and cause information to be late or slow, and you can lose a connection with them relatively easily because of the backups. Having access to different ISPs with different traffic patterns can help you avoid this problem.

Beyond this, you will need analytical tools and secondary information, which will be discussed a bit later in this chapter. The bottom line is that you will want to pick analytical tools and secondary information that best meet your style. Some people, for example, need an in-depth charting functionality in order to feel comfortable making a decision; to others, this is a useless feature. It is critical that you find a software package that has the best combination of what you need to feel informed. Very few companies can be everything to all people. Find one whose strengths match up with your needs.

Alternatively—and some very active direct access and day traders do this—you can choose to use the different strengths of all the different companies that are out there. Different execution platforms offer different functions and different secondary data. You just have to make sure the benefits of having multiple platforms outweigh their cost.

There are a few main qualities you should look for when deciding which direct access trading firm to use. One is speed of execution—the time difference between your placing of the order and its completion. Another is the functionality of the software's front end. The last is the reputation and history of the firm.

Speed is one of the most important—and most invisible—factors affecting the quality of your information and the success of your direct access trades. First, there is the speed of the quotes. This is the most fundamental area in which speed is needed—and the most commonly overlooked. It is something you do not really think about. You would not really consider the fact that the information you are looking at might be a second or two old if someone did not tell you to be mindful of it. But the difference 1, 2, or 3 seconds or even 4 or 5 seconds can make is enormous. If the information you are seeing is already late, if the information you are seeing is already outdated, then there is no possible way you can make a proper trading decision. You might get lucky, and the way you act on the information may still be relevant, but essentially, you are not really making a decision; you are gambling. If it is not timely, the information you are using to make a decision is not valid.

Second, there is the speed of your execution ability. This includes not only how fast an order gets routed but also how fast an order is routed in the most efficient possible manner. This is where "intelligent" or "smart" order routing technologies come into play. Smart routing involves the ability to make effective decisions very, very quickly. There are a number of criteria used to make such decisions. The most fundamental is an algorithm that drives how an order is routed, and if this is slow— if that takes 2 seconds to make a decision, then it is too late. Once again, the information that is being used is 2 seconds old. It is just too slow. The market can change drastically in 2 seconds. You have to deal in milliseconds in order for a decision to be made properly.

A routing system needs to be able to take multiple, dynamic variables and consider them in the context of speed, liquidity, and cost of execution. It needs to look at an order, make a millisecond decision as to how an order should be routed based on those variables, and route the order properly. This is the only way to achieve the goal of routing an order in the most efficient possible way as fast as possible.

Another important quality to look for when choosing a direct access firm is functionality and appearance of the front end. Many trading systems look extremely similar, so it is important to do careful research and to understand what the differences in systems are. This is so because the front end is your window to the market, your window to the trading world. It is what gives you the ability to process all the information needed to make viable trading decisions. Front-end software is key because it takes information and organizes it in a fashion that is quickly processable. It automatically sorts through information and presents it on one screen so that traders can intuitively react to it.

The front end needs to be constantly innovative about how information is fed to the trader. The use of colors, the use of fonts, and the simplicity of design are extremely important. Traders are looking at data constantly. The data are complicated; they are real-time, streaming, dynamic data and they come all day long. The goal of the front end is to make the processing of information quicker and more intuitive to enable the user to make a better, faster trading decision.

If the front end does not provide traders with the right environment— if it makes mistakes or, as one trader says, it "shines too much" and is not focused enough—an information overload can occur. Instead of having a disciplined approach to front-end design, a lot of software tries to be all things to all people and does not make any decisions about what is important and what is not important. This kind of software is often popular because it has broad appeal, but it does not usually boast very high success rates.

Thus the application you choose needs to have a front end that you are comfortable looking at. Is the software simple in terms of how it appears to you? Even though the software is often developed from tools meant for professional traders, it is modified to be accessible to retail customers. Instead of being a pseudoinstitutional product that requires two screens and 21-inch monitors and 50 different floating windows, it is usually a very simple, single interface. Direct access trading companies should take great pains to design tools that are attractive and unintimidating.

Most trading screens have three or four major areas. Firms have spent years figuring out how to keep one area from dominating any other and how to separate the sections without making the user feel like they are three or four different products. Little details like graphics, the way the mouse moves, and how much real estate your eyes have to cover between buying a stock and choosing a market maker are all crucial.

Therefore, make sure you understand all the information on the screen. Is it confusing to you? Is extraneous information shown? Is everything that you need right there and easy to see? Even with a simple, easy-to-read screen, it is possible to get overwhelmed with information. Therefore, it is extremely important that your firm's software can filter most of the physical information and only show you data that are pertinent to you. (Of course, it is the filtering of the potential trades that you have to do yourself that is more difficult and even more essential. Level II access is a powerful tool. If you harness the power and use it correctly, it can help you a lot. Used recklessly, it can lose you a lot of money.)

A final quality to consider when selecting a direct access firm is the company's history and reputation. Because direct access trading is so new, a firm's history could be only 2 years long. The important thing is to avoid a company that is right out of the gate, that has never processed a brokerage report or had to help customers go through taxes. A direct access trading firm needs to be able to do more than just help you buy and sell stock.

You should have no problems with trades appearing (or not appearing) in your account, for example. If you pick a reputable company whose entire business is trading, you can safeguard this. In contrast, a company whose main business is Web auction systems and which all of a sudden decides to get into the online trading world because it is hot is not a good choice. When you use an experienced company with a good reputation, you are guaranteeing yourself back-end support, account support, broker support, and the other benefits of hard-won knowledge.

In fact, many people feel that the best way to measure a firm is by the success of its traders. There is a reason why successful traders go to a certain firm. Part of this reason is the discipline in the front-end software the company uses, and a lot of it is the fact that success begets success. As one trader says, "You know that something right is going on—something right is happening in that environment."

Another key factor to consider when choosing a direct access system is which option offers you the most connectivity. Look for the option that gives you a single window to the greatest amount of liquidity and direct access. If you can connect through a firm that offers a consolidated market, a consolidated portal, and a window into that liquidity, you are all set. This is the only way to benefit from all the liquidity pools that are out there. Otherwise, you will be participating in 15 to 20 percent of the market at most. You need to have access to a provider of a *pool* of technology. The connectivity to the different markets provided by the direct access company you are using is important as well.

Although some people think so, it is not necessarily a bad thing for a direct access firm to be aligned with a particular ECN—as long as the firm allows you to use other ECNs as well. In fact, an alliance with a particular ECN can give a firm the ability to route orders in an even more efficient way. This is so because the ECN can act as a place to hold orders that are not currently marketable and a place from which to route that order if and when it does become marketable.

In other words, an ECN gives traders the ability to place limit orders that are not marketable. And when the order does become marketable, if there is no internal match for it, the firm can route it immediately and get it executed in the fastest and most efficient manner possible.

The reliability of the system cannot be underestimated either. The challenge is to ensure reliability in such a way that it does not compromise speed. As one software designer says, "The problem with many systems out there is that they don't understand that if you don't have speed, you don't have anything. If you have an extremely reliable, fault-tolerant system with no speed, it's great, but no one's going to use it. The challenge is to be able to . . . [offer] a fault-tolerant, reliable system which is as fast as hell."

Both the speed and the reliability of a direct access system are critical. You cannot compromise speed, but at the same time you need to make sure that your system is reliable and does not go down.

Consistency should be a priority, too. Your system should be accessible to you at all times. It should not crash; you should not have problems getting brokerage reports; you should not be kicked off. Most all, you should not suffer slow execution. Slow execution defeats the purpose of using a direct level II system.

Accurate position monitoring is important as well. Tradescape Pro and similar tools will tell you how much money you are gaining or losing from a certain position. Charts and records for following your movements help you evaluate what you did and why you did it. Account information shows how much money you have, how much money you have in use, how much stock you own, how much money you have made on positions you have closed out, and how much money you have lost on positions you currently have open. Both market information and personalized information are presented to the investor in a very organized manner.

Finally, a word about analytical tools: Although analytical tools are not something you *need* to trade, they can be helpful. Since there is some confusion on the topic, the best place to explain them is probably here.

There is a simple difference between trading tools and analytical tools: Trading tools include real-time information, like quotes and intraday stock movement data, as well as the devices used to actually execute an actual order. Analytical tools, in contrast, are geared toward secondary information, not trading information, and have nothing to do with executing an order. They are used as information filters on the market, on groups of stock, or on one stock in particular. Analytical tools help traders shore up their trading decisions with information about what is happening in a company, movement in a particular stock, and comparisons between that stock and other stocks that have moved similarly or are in the same industry group. Examples include Bloomberg and First Alert, even Yahoo! Finance. But these tools do not have anything to do directly with trading.

Although analytical tools are important, they should not show up on your trading window. Your window should be geared toward trading decisions only; crossing analytical and trading functions can affect the functionality of the trading platform.

The information on your trading screen should be simplified, streamlined, and directly relevant. It should feature position management and level II quote information and include stock picking filters and other tools that give you the ability to filter out stocks based on movement, price, spread, performance, volume, and other factors. Personal lists let traders watch movement and see stocks color-coded by person, industry group, and other specifications.

Chart information also can be important, but if you have too much charting information, you have too much news, too much analysis on your trading software. The result is a loss of functionality. Software should be strictly separated into trading and analytical tools.

Luckily for the consumer, companies have designed and continue to design direct access tools with ease of use as their top priority. Even when tools change or new features are added on the front end, the user experience does not change. All changes are on the back end, so there is no intimidation factor.

Tradescape Pro and other similar trading products are very intelligent but easy-to-comprehend pieces of software. At the core, they are execution platforms. They take information from Nasdaq, which is sent to you, the individual investor, through the main Tradescape system and then filter that data so that you see the correct information. *Correct information* means pertinent data on a stock, level II displays, charts, the ability to monitor your position, the ability to buy and sell, and the ability to access numerous ECNs (see Figures 3–1 through 3–4).

The end result is a constant flow of the proper information coming in a timely manner and a great deal of liquidity, allowing you to get in and out of stocks. The tools are designed to appear simple, but the back end is very sophisticated.

Most direct access trading software is available in a number of different versions. One is an HTML (Hypertext Markup Language) version, which is Web-based and is very basic. It works similarly to a Schwab or E*TRADE trade. The other is a Java applet version. The applet can be accessed from anywhere in the world. This means that you can trade from anywhere—whether you are at home, at the office, or in a library or a cybercafé somewhere in the Bahamas. This is extremely convenient. Now is the first time that such sophisticated capabilities have been made available to the retail investor.

The applet version opens up with an Internet browser, which enables streaming information. There is no download to the hard drive. Unlike with the HTML version, you can update your front end—or the version of your software—overnight. The software does not sit on your hard drive; you never have to download a new version of it. Instead, it updates automatically. This is better for you the customer—as well as for the trading firm whose software you are using (the firm does not have to worry about people having an execution system that has a huge bug or problem in it sitting on its hard drive).

Java applet-based systems really leverage the convenience of the Internet. In the past, since the systems lived on one particular computer—say, your laptop or your personal computer in your den—there were limitations on its use. The applet systems are much more convenient and allow users to keep up with the front-end software as it changes and updates.

Right now there are many different technologies and many different

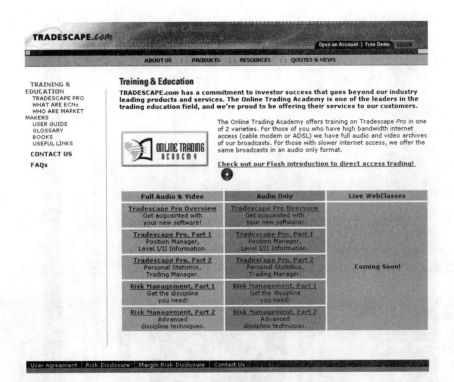

Figure 3-1.   Tradescape.com training and education. (*Courtesy of Tradescape.*)

platforms, which causes a high level of fragmentation. But this is the way that most technology and other business improvements start out: Industries start off extremely fragmented, and then companies begin to merge and consolidate, and standards emerge. Then there is a race to the finish. The companies and the technologies that have the most vision as to how they see the innovations adapting and improving are the ones who win in the end. In the case of direct access technologies, the ones that provide the simplest solutions to the most complex questions are the ones that will end up on top.

Take Tradescape, one of the most well-respected direct access firms out there. Software developers at this firm see the need to consolidate liquidity pools and "create an ocean of liquidity through which users have a single interface, simple single interface" as the top priority. The goal of the firm is to provide a learning-based, dynamic environment that provides intelligent order routing. Users should feel comfortable letting

TRADESCAPE.com

Open an Account | Free Demo | LOGIN

ABOUT US :: PRODUCTS :: RESOURCES :: QUOTES & NEWS

ONLINE TRADING
FEATURES
PRICING
GETTING STARTED
USER GUIDE
FREE SIMULATOR
WHAT'S NEW

PROFESSIONAL
FEATURES

LEVEL II QUOTES
FEATURES
PRICING
GETTING STARTED

Free Simulator

Tradescape Challenge is a powerful simulation of our online trading technology. It's easy to use, and there's no risk involved. Whether you've traded before or you're just getting started, this is your chance to experience all the features that Tradescape PRO* has to offer:

- Level II Quotes (delayed 15 minutes)– dynamic market maker and ECN movements

- Smart Order Routing Technology™ - scans the market for the best possible price

- Electronic Communication Portal™ technology - connectivity to the top market makers and ECNs in each stock.

- Dynamic market indicators - measures of strength and volatility

- Fast Executions

▶ SIGN UP FOR TRADESCAPE CHALLENGE

*The actual trading platform has some additional features, but this game will allow you to sample our product and get a feel for trading with Tradescape.com.

User Agreement | Risk Disclosure | Margin Risk Disclosure | Contact Us

Figure 3-2. Tradescape.com free simulator. (*Courtesy of Tradescape.*)

TRADESCAPE.com

ABOUT US :: PRODUCTS :: RESOURCES :: QUOTES & NEWS

ONLINE TRADING
FEATURES
PRICING
GETTING STARTED
USER GUIDE
FREE SIMULATOR
WHAT'S NEW

PROFESSIONAL
FEATURES

LEVEL II QUOTES
FEATURES
PRICING
GETTING STARTED

Professional Trading

Soon to be released online:

Lightspeed is the next generation of our FirstLevel™ trading software that is used by thousands of professional on-site traders. This stand-alone trading platform will allow remote customers to experience the superior software functionality and performance exclusively available to our on-site trading veterans.

To learn more about Lightspeed and when it will be available online please contact us at:
Lightspeed@tradescape.com

See Lightspeed in action

Learn more about Lightspeed's features

- **Direct Connections to ECNs and Nasdaq:** Gain a competitive edge with faster information and faster trades.

- **Smart Order Routing:** Seek the best venue for executing your trade.

- **Customization and Filter Consoles:** Choose the data you want, the way you want to see it.

- **Thermographs:** Track the direction and intensity of market movements.

- **ECP Book:** View the best bids and offers from every ECN, centralized in a single book.

- **Latency Console:** Know the speed of each ECN before you trade.

Figure 3-3. Tradescape.com professional trading. (*Courtesy of Tradescape.*)

35

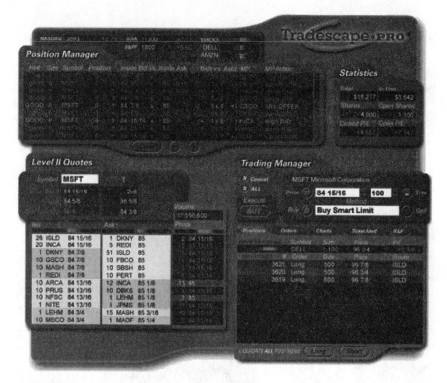

Figure 3-4. Tradescape Pro position manager. (*Courtesy of Tradescape.*)

"smart" ordering systems make trading decisions, even splicing up orders and routing them to the most appropriate places. The ordering systems should find the cheapest, fastest, and most efficient execution method by determining where liquidity is naturally available.

The next step for Tradescape and other direct access firms is to provide customized front-end solutions for different types of traders and order flow types. Direct access traders range from individuals on E*TRADE who want only level I information, need to be able to execute based on that very basic information, and require a streaming front-end tool to do so to institutional brokers who place huge orders and need tools to help them interface directly into the market. People want different levels of intelligence as to how an order is routed, as well as different levels of connectivity to the different exchanges. All this involves tweaking at the back end that the customer does not see. The race among firms is to see who can be the end-to-end solution provider for all kinds of companies and all kinds of individuals.

Tradescape's and other firms' mission is to make trading accessible for everyone. Their goal is to offer all their traders—institutional, in-house, day, electronic, and online—the best and most tools as well as the fastest way to access those tools. In addition, their ECN efforts should bring a lot more liquidity to investors and allow individuals easier access to that liquidity.

Right now, most firms offer only level II quote products geared toward traders who need or use level II quotes to make trading decisions. The products have a position manager window that gives people the ability to track multiple positions in multiple stocks simultaneously and color codes movement based on whether it is good or bad for various positions. It uses the English language to logically explain what is happening in level II quotes, but it is geared toward the more sophisticated, active online trader.

Now the firms are working on new level I products that should appear on the market shortly. These are geared toward users who want sharing information and real-time data but who do not need level II quotes to make trading decisions. This type of product is for the mass market, people who want to benefit from the latest technology but do not need the second-by-second information used by extremely active and day traders. These are investors who are happy with level I information but want to be able to benefit from the execution ability, the back end, of direct access tools. The products will have a level I quote board, which will show the last trade, net change for the day, the best bid, the best ask, amount of shares traded for the day, the high, the low, and other data for any stock. The board also will have order entry capabilities to the firm's back end, intraday charting functionality, some position management ability, and a few level II positions. The idea is to create a streamlined product that covers a lot of the basics. When this happens, direct access tools will truly be accessible to everyone.

SUMMARY

The hardware and technological requirements are very similar to those of online investing. Depending on the direct access trading firm you use, there also may be software requirements, although many are going to

Web-based systems. The main difference is that the interface you are using to place your trades is going to be very different. For the first time you will have access to a whole other layer of data that shows what the inside players are doing within a stock. The key is more to spend time customizing your user interface so that you have all the pertinent information you need on one screen and do not need to waste time eyeballing information that is of no use to you. For new direct access traders, one of the hardest things to do in the beginning is to not get overloaded with information. Experienced direct access traders often tell stories about new traders who are paralyzed with information and cannot execute trades because they become so bogged down with so many different pieces of information. Almost every successful trader has a very different trading style and uses very different pieces of information to place trades. Some only use 1 or 2 pieces of information, whereas others may have a checklist of 20 items that must coexist before they execute a trade. The key is customizing exactly the information you need to be confident in your trade. This obviously will change over time, but you need to use the software to give you the information you need, and only the information you need, in the quickest time period possible.

Experiment with what you currently have as a computer before you run out and buy a new one. Speed, however, is one of the direct access trader's best weapons, so make sure there is no lag time in terms of placing trades or receiving data. Especially if you are making intraday trades, this can be costly. However, if you are making longer-term trades, you can get away with a lot more from a technological standpoint. There are thousands of different computers in the marketplace, and even some direct access trading firms have relationships with specific vendors. Retailers such as Dell and Gateway also have programs where you can lease computers from anywhere from $25 to $55 a month, and this can be a great way to get started if your cash flow is a bit low.

If you are going to trade at an actual direct access trading firm, you also want to do your own homework regarding their equipment. Second-hand computers from 1995 just are not going to cut it in the direct access trading world. One of the major advantages of going to a firm is that it should have the best equipment and connection speeds and provide an environment that is conducive to trading. A lot of traders swear by this trading environment and could never think of trading without others screaming around them. Many feel that interacting with other direct access traders helps them to find out about new stocks and get another perspective on what is happening with the market or a stock in general. Others prefer to trade out of the comfort of their own homes and be left to peace and quiet so that they can concentrate. However, if you are going to a direct access trading firm, make sure that it has top-notch equipment. This is definitely one of the red flag areas I talked about earlier to keep an eye on.

And finally, talk to other direct access traders. Other traders are usually your best source of information when deciding which computer, software, or modem speed to use. Although each one is a different trader and has different preferences, they will be able to give you real insight as to the success or lack thereof they have had with various systems. Just remember, however, that since each of them does have an individual trading style, the responses are likely to be varied. Traders are usually very vehement regarding their trading systems and will definitely give you their honest opinion, but always take it with a grain of salt. The best way is often if you can spend some time seeing how a computer handles the data and the connection speed before you make the purchase.

All and all, it should not cost you too much to get set up with direct access trading tools. Worst-case scenario, if you trade from home and want to get set up with a new computer, DSL line, and furnish your home office, it should still not run you more than a couple of thousand dollars. Get set up right from the start so that you can spend your time where you should—on learning how to make money using direct access trading tools.

QUESTIONS TO ASK YOURSELF

1   How important is it for me to have a fast connection to the Internet such as DSL or a T1 line?

2   Am I going to trade from home or go to a direct access trading firm?

3   What are the advantages and disadvantages of each?

4   Do I need to be set up at home as well if I do end up going to a direct access trading firm?

5   What type of direct access trading software is best suited to my needs?

6   What direct access traders can I talk to to get their feedback on computer hardware and software?

7   Do I need to go out and buy a computer, or is what I have sufficient?

8   How much can I afford to spend on direct access trading equipment?

SYMBOLS AND TERMS

Knowing some of the symbols and terms used in direct access trading not only will help you to more feel at home with trading lingo but also will help you understand how the actual execution of your trades takes place. If you already understand how the electronic markets work, you may want to skip this chapter. If not—or if you would like a review or a clearer explanation—this chapter is key.

BULLS, BEARS, AND OTHER ANIMALS

What is meant by a *bull* market and what is meant by a *bear* market? And what causes each? Before you can understand the types of markets, it is important to understand how shares of stock change hands and what causes their prices to move up or down. Many people believe that a stock's price changes because there are more buyers than sellers, or vice versa. This is not really the case, because for any transaction to occur, there must be both a buyer and a seller; there need to be equal numbers of shares being bought and sold. Instead, price changes have to do with supply and demand. For example, when a stock's price rises, this means that all the stock available for a certain price has been bought and that buyers are willing to buy at the next highest level at which the stock is being offered. Because the stock is in high demand, buyers will buy all the stock at the first price level and then will go to the next one. This can occur at consecutively higher price levels, which causes the stock's price to rise.

When you buy a stock expecting its price to rise, you hold what is called a *long* position in the stock; you own the stock in hopes that it will move up so that you can sell it at an even higher price. Interestingly, you also can make a profit by buying a stock in expectations that its price will go down; this is called *shorting* a stock or holding a *short* position. In this case, you borrow shares of stock from a broker and sell them in anticipation of buying them back later at a lower price and keeping the difference.

Put simply, a *bull* market is one in which prices are generally rising and that most gains are to be made by going long. The current bull market has been going on for almost 20 years, with exception of a few minor corrections. There are many reasons for this, including the development of tools that have allowed individual investors to access the markets directly (the subject of this book). Other reasons include the popularity of mutual funds, lower savings account interest rates (which prompts people to invest in the stock market instead), and the investing of the baby boomers, who are in their prime earning years right now.

A *bear* market, in contrast, trends toward lower prices. It is generally defined as a market that retreats at least 20 percent from its previous high. Bear markets do not usually last nearly as long as bull markets do, but they often drop two to three times as fast. This is so because fear is a stronger emotion than optimism, which means that prices fall faster and more deeply than they rise, which they do in stages. Thus, while money is made more often by going long, greater and quicker profits actually can be made by going short. Most financial publications, such as the *Wall Street Journal, Barron's*, and *Investors Business Daily,* have monthly sections listing the stocks that currently have the greatest potential for shorting.

Finally, it is amusing to know where the names *bull* and *bear* markets came from. Long ago, *bear skin jobbers* were known for selling bear skins that they did not own because the bears had not yet been caught. This term came to describe short sellers, who sell shares they do not own, clearly hoping that the market will go down. Since both bull and bear baiting were once popular sports, *bulls* came to be seen as the opposite of *bears*. Bulls buy stock in anticipation that the market will rise.

THE EXCHANGES: THE NEW YORK STOCK EXCHANGE AND THE NASDAQ

The New York Stock Exchange (NYSE) is the largest stock exchange in the world and is what most people traditionally think of when they think of the stock market. Many of the country's best and most established companies, such as General Electric (GE) and IBM, are listed here. The Dow Jones Industrial Average (DJIA), the most famous market index in the world, comprises 30 of the leading companies listed on the NYSE, including GE, General Motors, and Johnson and Johnson. Because each company in the index represents a major U.S. industry, the DJIA is often used as a measure of the overall health of the U.S. economy. It is a measure of market sentiment because its numbers, especially milestone ones, are watched closely by both the public and professional investors.

The NYSE is an auction-oriented market, which means that its prices are determined by competitive bidding between traders who represent buyers and sellers. Individuals or firms called *specialists* coordinate this buying and selling between bidders and offerers by matching them up, are responsible for maintaining fairness between the two parties, and try to ensure constant liquidity in the stocks they represent to maintain organization and fairness between buyers and sellers. An auction market operates in an actual physical place, and you must have a seat on the actual trading floor to participate.

The Nasdaq (National Association of Securities Dealers Automated Quotation System), in contrast, is a dealer market or a negotiated market. This means that instead of one actual trading floor, transactions take place over a computer network consisting of innumerable trading terminals from which bids and offers are made. It is a virtual market instead of a physical one.

Firms called *dealers* or *market makers* (companies that represent individual stocks) and traders compete for the best prices. Orders are not routed through a single entity like a specialist but instead are posted as bids and offers on an electronic network that people can see and take advantage of. However, placing orders directly on the Nasdaq is more complicated than placing orders on the NYSE because the Nasdaq employs a number of different routing systems, which will be discussed later in this chapter.

One thing that is important for direct access traders to understand is that the Nasdaq has two levels of information that can be accessed. *Level I information* shows the best current buying and selling orders, known as the basic *inside market.* Level I is used mostly by stockbrokers and online investors who are not particularly concerned about getting extremely quick order execution because they plan to hold their stocks longer than a couple of minutes or hours, like day traders. *Level II information,* in contrast, is extremely important for day traders and very active online investors. Level II information allows you to see what is happening beneath the inside market, including all the buying and selling pressure by various groups on the stock.

Because of the higher level of speculation that occurs on the Nasdaq (the companies listed on it are not as established as those on the NYSE), it is considered more volatile than the NYSE and is particularly popular with day traders. The Nasdaq can experience 20-point or greater swings in a single day. It is, however, the second largest stock exchange in the United States and is home to most of the technology stocks and the stocks of other emerging companies. Therefore, it is seen as an indicator of the health of the technology sector of the economy. You can tell the difference between stocks listed on the NYSE and those listed on the Nasdaq because NYSE stocks are represented by one-, two-, or three-letter symbols and Nasdaq stocks are represented by four- or five-letter symbols.

A number of important indexes are derived from the NYSE and the Nasdaq. The Standard & Poors 500 (S&P500) Index is a benchmark of the 500 largest stocks, by market value, that are listed on the NYSE or the Nasdaq. The performance of mutual funds is usually measured against this index. The Nasdaq 100 is a market value-weighted index that measures the 100 largest U.S.-based nonfinancial companies that are traded on the Nasdaq. Computer and software stocks make up 63 percent of this index's value, and telecommunications stocks make up another 18 percent. Major representatives on the Nasdaq 100 include Microsoft, Intel, Dell, Cisco, MCI/Worldcom, Amazon, and Yahoo. Nasdaq itself says that these 100 stocks have a 94 percent correlation with the Nasdaq as a whole, which in turn reflects the technology market at large.

SPECIALISTS

To better understand how the NYSE and the Nasdaq work, it is important to understand the role of specialists and market makers, who facilitate and profit from the transactions on these exchanges. Before this, however, it is necessary to understand what creates the forces that allow market makers and specialists to profit in the first place.

The market is an ever-dynamic situation. New buyers and sellers constantly enter the market with new *bids* (the price at which a party is willing to buy stock) and *asks* (the price at which a party is willing to sell stock). These, in turn, cause both the price of a stock and the volume of transactions to change.

The best current buying price and order size, or the highest price at which one entity is willing to buy stock from another, is known as the *inside bid*. The best current selling price and order size, or the lowest price at which one entity is willing to sell stock to another, is known as the *inside ask*. Together, the inside bid and the inside ask make up what is known as the *inside market*, or the *quote*. The difference between the inside bid and inside ask is known as the *spread*.

On the NYSE and other auction markets, a specialist firm—or a specialist—is assigned to be in charge of the transactions in each stock. All transactions on that stock have to go through that specialist. There can be more than one stock assigned to each specialist but no more than one specialist to each stock. Specialists act as auctioneers and match buy and sell orders by adjusting prices to meet supply and demand. This can be difficult when the market is moving fast, because all kinds of orders—of different kinds, sizes, and prices—are placed. In exchange, specialists get to keep the spread on all the orders they buy and sell out of their own inventory.

The reason specialists can buy and sell from their own inventory is because their job is to *make a market* in the stocks they represent. This means that not only must they make sure the market in a stock is fair and organized, but they also must make sure there are buyers and sellers of the stocks they cover at all times. In fact, if someone wants to buy or sell stock and there is no one else to do it, the specialist *must* do so from its own account. This ensures that there is always stability and liquidity in the stock even if there are no buyers and sellers on the public market.

So how do specialists make money—what is in it for them? First, as mentioned, they can profit from the difference between the buying and selling prices, or the spread. Second, whenever they fulfill customer orders, whether from large institutions or individual customers, they mark up stocks, or charge a commission. Third, specialists can trade in the interest of their own accounts if they feel strongly about which way a stock is moving.

Most frequently, specialists profit by charging a markup for always having the stock on hand. Specialists will always sell you a stock at a fractionally higher price than they will buy it from you. This is legal because it is considered a fair tradeoff; again, because they risk their own capital to maintain an orderly market and act as both buyers and sellers when required, they are allowed to make money by skimming off some money from the spread. (The amount of the spread is determined by the volatility of the stock; the more volatile a stock is, the wider is its spread.)

In addition, because they must risk their own money to make sure there is always someone to take the other side of a customer's trade, specialists are also allowed to take their own positions in stocks. In return for the disadvantage of always having to buy or sell the stock if there is an order and no one else to fill it, they get the advantage of knowing before anyone else what direction the stock is trending in—and are allowed to profit from this knowledge by selling from their own positions. This still works well for the public because specialists are required to always give preference to customers' orders over their own.

MARKET MAKERS

Market makers are similar to specialists in that it is their job to represent a stock to the public. They must post a buying and selling price for the stocks they cover at all times and trade from their own accounts to fill customer orders if necessary. They are also allowed to trade the stock from their own accounts to make a profit.

Like specialists, market makers are intermediaries in buying and selling. Unlike on the NYSE, however, where each stock has only one specialist, on the Nasdaq—where market makers operate—more than one firm can represent each stock. In fact, many stocks on the Nasdaq have 10 to 20 market makers assigned to them. Each market maker must simply guarantee that it will provide a two-sided market at all times, meaning that it will post a price at which it will sell and another at which it will buy.

Because so many market makers can represent the same stock, they compete to provide the best price to the public. Maintaining liquidity means that they must feel out the market and adjust their prices until they reach a point at which buying and selling occur.

Like specialists, market makers hold a risky position but stand to make lots of money. This, again, is because of the bid-ask spread. Market makers always must have a price at which they will buy and sell each of the stocks they represent in order to guarantee that customers will always be able to execute a trade in a stock. Market makers actually keep the markets running. In return for this responsibility, they get to profit from the spread on trades, since their buy prices will always be lower than their sell prices.

As on the NYSE, the spreads are biggest and the market makers can make the most money when the market is most volatile. The difference between a market maker's buy and sell prices is larger (it can be as high as $1); the firms do this in order to protect themselves in case the market moves against them.

Because Nasdaq does not have just one firm handling and organizing each stock's order, it can be hard to know what is really out there to buy or sell. Just because a market maker posts 1000 shares, for example, does not mean that it does not have many more shares to sell. A market maker that keeps posting shares consecutively may have a huge lot to sell but not want to show its hand for fear of causing the price to fall. And there may be many more market makers out there selling that stock. However, the market maker system is not anonymous; the names of the firms are out there, posted on the Small Order Execution System (SOES), so you can at least try to figure out what they are trying to do.

Also, the Nasdaq system does not require market makers to display block orders—or orders of more than 10,000 shares or $25,000—which can be frustrating because it is big orders like these which cause major price movements.

Furthermore, there is not one entity entirely in charge of a stock and to whom complaints about fairness can go. As a result, there have been charges of price fixing and other unfairness by market makers as a group over the years. Regardless of whether or not these charges are true, because of the way it is organized, the market maker system tends to make for more volatility than the specialist system.

SMALL ORDER EXECUTION SYSTEM (SOES)

What allows you as an individual trader to benefit from the market maker model is something called the *Small Order Execution System* (SOES).

This is an automated system for bypassing brokers when placing orders of up to 1000 shares of a Nasdaq stock. Because it ensures the electronic routing and automatic execution of your order to the market maker offering the best price, SOES is what assures you as a small trader that your orders will be filled. It is also what assures day traders that their orders will be filled instantaneously (which, in turn, allows them to take greater risks, since they can exit any stock in a matter of seconds).

There are two types of orders on SOES. One is a *limit order,* which is an order to make a transaction only at a specified price—usually the current inside market or better. If no stock is available at that price, your order will not be filled. Limit orders are used by people who have decided the price at which they are willing to trade; buyers or sellers who place limit orders will not buy or sell for a bit more than they qualified.

Limit orders are the preferred form of ordering for professional day traders, who need to use them to make profits. This is so because limit orders determine the ends of the spread, making sure that highest bid and lowest offer are posted. Thus the bid-ask spreads displayed on level II quote systems (to be discussed later in this chapter) are determined by those placing this type of order.

A *market order,* in contrast, is an order for execution at the best price available when the order reaches the marketplace. Market orders are used by people who really want a stock and are therefore willing to pay a little more for the guarantee of getting it. You do not negotiate; instead, you agree to pay or sell for whatever price the market is currently offering. And unlike day traders, you do not care about getting it instantaneously. This is how most of the public buys and sells stock.

The advantage of placing a market order is that your order will almost always be filled, since you are not specifying any particular price. The disadvantage is that you are somewhat at the mercy of the seller; most of the time, using a market order means that you as the buyer are agreeing to seller's terms. This is how Wall Street firms that sell stocks make so much money.

Nonetheless, it is important to understand that limit orders—and SOES in general—are not really for the average investor or for those who plan to buy and hold.

The National Association of Securities Dealers (NASD) created SOES as a result of the 1987 stock market crash. The idea was to help both market makers and individual investors to get their orders executed during a high-volume or low-liquidity market. More specifically, SOES gave individual investors the ability to get an order of 1000 shares or less of a Nasdaq stock filled—immediately—at the inside market.

Until 1987, there was no mandatory execution system. This meant that when the market crashed, market makers simply withdrew their bids and asks, which drastically reduced liquidity. Market makers simply did not have to fill orders, which put small investors at a great disadvantage.

Therefore, in mid-1988, NASD made SOES participation mandatory for all Nasdaq market makers. Now all market makers had to execute any SOES order or give it to another market maker within a certain time frame or face stiff penalties. Market makers also were required to honor the quotes that were in effect at the time the order was placed, something they had not had to do in the past. The bottom line: Market makers had to provide constant liquidity in their stocks.

One immediate result of this system was the creation of something called *SOES trading*. Traders saw that they could watch the market closely and enter and leave it extremely quickly for fast, short-term gains. (Sound familiar?) It was not long before market makers complained, and starting in August 1988, the NASD formulated a number of rules to constrain this practice.

The first was the 1000-share rule. This rule declared *batching,* or simultaneously placing several 1000-share orders for a stock in one account or through multiple accounts, illegal. This is still a rule to this day, because it keeps SOES a system for the small investor.

The 5-minute rule works in conjunction with the 1000-share rule. This rule provides that any trades entered within a 5-minute period in accounts controlled by a single interest shall be considered "a single investment decision." The idea is to prevent people from entering a number of 1000-share orders in rapid succession to make it look like they were separate decisions. Both the 5-minute rule and the 1000-share rule apply only to a single stock.

Next came the professional trader rule, which defined a *professional trader* as any account in which five or more trades took place in one day or in which a "professional trading pattern" through SOES could be established. Anyone determined to be a professional trader by these definitions would then be subject to the same regulations and restrictions as true professionals. (By end of 1991, there was enough of a reaction from SOES traders to the professional trader rule, who said that the rule unfairly protected market makers and kept the market from being competitive and liquid, that a number of legal arguments and appeals were put in motion. By 1993, the professional trader rule was repealed.)

Another rule, the short-sale rule, was instituted in January 1995. It disallows short sales in Nasdaq at or below the inside bid when the current inside bid is below the previous one. In other words, you cannot sell a stock short unless the last movement in its bid was upward.

More recently, in 1997, the Securities and Exchange Commission (SEC) created new order-handling rules that require market makers to always show the best price at which a stock is being offered. In the past, market makers often neglected to show quotes and limit orders priced better than those at which they wanted to trade stock. Or they did not report transactions until after the market closed so that people could not find out the price of their transactions until after the fact. Both these practices created unusually high spreads. Since the order-handling rules were instituted, however, spreads have been reduced by more than 25 percent.

Finally, the actual-size rule was approved in 1998. It says that market makers, when placing a customer limit order, only have to post 100 shares, rather than 1000, to make a market. (In the past, market makers had to place orders for 1000 shares at a time.) This allows the market makers to post the actual size of a limit order instead of making them responsible for trading a total of 1000 shares when they only have an order for 100.

ELECTRONIC COMMUNICATION NETWORKS

Electronic communication networks (ECNs) are networks that allow traders and institutions to post buy and sell orders directly to the Nasdaq. They are the main way market makers use to trade more shares than those allowed on SOES. Instead of showing the identity of the people or institutions posting bids, offers, and order size, as on SOES, each ECN reflects the total sum of everyone using it to trade. Individual bids and asks are absorbed into a larger amount. (This is why market makers sometimes use ECNs to maintain anonymity.) Therefore, the number of shares posted to trade on an ECN is more a reflection of actual interest in a stock than are individual market maker bids and asks on SOES.

Because ECNs are networks of traders instead of firms that represent stocks, they are not responsible for providing liquidity or taking the opposite side of any trade like specialists and market makers are. At the same time, ECNs do actually allow individuals to help make the market because, like market makers, you can enter an order at any price. It does not have to be at the inside bid or ask. It can be higher, lower, or between the spread.

People like ECNs because they enable small investors—and not just large institutions—to post bids and asks directly to the market. This encourages more liquidity, more competition, and therefore better prices. ECNs also allow you to place buy and sell orders more easily and with more flexibility than SOES.

Another advantage of ECNs is in selling short. On SOES, you have to make sure that there is an *upbid* (meaning that the last movement of a stock must have been in an upward direction) before you can short. On ECNs, however, since you can make your own market, you can create your own upbid by offering to buy a small amount of shares for $\frac{1}{16}$ more than current price. Then you can short the stock.

ECNs also help you avoid what are known as *headfakes*. Headfakes occur on SOES when a market maker posts shares at a price better than the current inside market in order to trick people into thinking the market is moving in a direction it is not. (The idea is to then remove the shares before anyone actually decides to trade them.) Big orders on ECNs, in contrast, are likely to be more authentic because if the fake price is actually traded on before it can be withdrawn, the market maker or trader could be stuck with the full order (unlike on SOES, where you can get only 1000 shares). Thus the risk of making a headfake on an ECN is just too great.

However, while ECNs are more flexible and reliable in some ways than SOES, they involve more risk if you do not use them correctly. On ECNs, there is no guarantee that someone will buy or sell at your posted price. Only SOES allows you a guaranteed exit. Thus day traders, for example, even though they can buy more than 1000 shares on an ECN, generally will not because they can only *sell* 1000 shares on SOES (every 5 minutes). They use ECNs to buy and sell when making profits and use SOES to exit when things are not going their way. Both tools are important.

Another disadvantage of ECNs is that you cannot place stop orders. This is so because sell orders are usually placed just below the stock's current price so that the seller can get rid of the stock if the price starts to fall.

The costs of using an ECN vary from nothing to about $7.50 a trade;

right now there are nine different ECNs to choose from. One of the most popular is SelectNet, the ECN run by Nasdaq. SelectNet is efficient, quick, and cheap. It also lets you preference certain market makers, which means that only those market makers will be told how many shares you want to trade.

Another widely used ECN is Instinet (INCA), a private ECN operated by Reuters. It was used originally to let institutional investors show bids and offers to each other anonymously and is now the biggest and most liquid ECN. It and SelectNet are mostly used by market makers, who like the fact that it allows them to place orders outside the inside market. (Bids and asks at each given price are lined up as they are received. Placing orders in advance allows you to buy on bid or sell when stock begins trading there, which in turn eliminates the spread.) At this point, institutional investors can trade after hours on Instinet. Its global trading system matches up orders with one another and does not require an actual exchange to complete transactions. However, after-hours trading on Instinet is still very expensive and does not yet include individual investors. SelectNet has a similar after-hours service.

The main disadvantage of Instinet is that while order execution is as efficient on other ECNs, trade reporting is slow. It can take up to a minute for a trade to be confirmed. Day traders need confirmations much faster than this.

Island is an ECN operated by discount brokerage Datek Securities. Advantages of Island are that trade reporting and execution are almost instantaneous. Also, people who use island are almost all noninstitutional, and because of their naïveté, this ECN can offer some of the best opportunities to profit.

Archipelago has fast order execution and automated negotiation and allows you to place orders outside the inside market. You also can preference orders as with SelectNet and Instinet. This is the cheapest ECN, charging 50 cents per 1000 shares traded.

Bloomberg's Tradebook came out in 1999. It is a buy-side trading ECN that allows orders to be matched directly by customers themselves. Buy-side traders can either target all market makers and ECNs at specific prices or preference certain firms.

Recently, there has been talk about connecting all the ECNs (there are others besides those mentioned above), which currently stand alone. This would greatly increase liquidity. Right now, All-Tech's Attain links to Archipelago and Island and is planning on providing connections to Strike, REDIBook, and Brut. Bloomberg, Tradebook, Archipelago, REDIBook, and others are discussing linking systems after hours.

LEVEL II DATA

Most individuals are familiar with level I quotes. These are what are in the newspaper the following morning or what you can pull off of most investment Web sites. Level I quotes are like trading with only one part of the story. They show you a snapshot of the price for a particular stock. You do not get to see all the groups that are bidding different prices for the stock and the potential momentum driving the price one way or another. Level II data are the most important tool for direct access traders. Level II data or a level II quote system allows users to see more details of a stock's current price than a standard quotation system does. Level II shows bids and asks from market makers and individual investors trading on the different ECNs at any given time. It displays all the posted buyers and sellers of a stock, identifying them and specifying at what price and how many shares they are willing to trade. As prices rise and fall, bids and asks are cleared, and then higher or lower prices are shown. Real-time reports, known as *time & sales* or *prints,* confirm the trades, their price, and their size.

Usually only the more expensive quote systems include level II information, but it is very important information for very active traders—especially day traders—to have. Otherwise, they could miss changes in the market. Some places even allow individuals to purchase the level II quotes as a stand-alone product for anywhere from $79.95 to $150.00 a month. Although this may seem like a lot, the information it provides is well worth the expense. Other firms are even packaging it now with their software so that you can get it for even much less a month. Level II information helps investors to get a clearer picture of the stock, zero in on data better, and execute orders faster. It also tells them the direction in which the momentum is currently moving; they can see who has the upper hand by whether buyers are willing to meet sellers' prices or vice versa. Other clues are *override trades,* or trades beyond the current highest bid or ask, and the range and the amount of shares available at both the bid and the ask. However, it is important to remember that level II information is just a tool. It can help you anticipate price direction, but it cannot make you a better trader. It is essential to cross-reference data from level II with other sources.

You also should know that one disadvantage of trading from home is that your executions are almost always going to be a fraction of a second slower than those of large Wall Street firms. Thus, if you are looking at the same quotes, often what determines your success is speed. Therefore, you need to anticipate and not trade exactly at the moment everyone else is. You have to be a few seconds ahead. It is possible that if you wait for a stock's price to actually begin to rise and orders to flow in, yours will be the last order filled, at the worst price.

Even so, access to level II is obviously a valuable tool—it bridges much of the gap that used to exist between individual investors and professional traders. So how does level II work? Well, when prices rise, both the bid and the ask go up. Buyers raise the bid to show that they are willing to pay more, and sellers raise the ask in hopes of selling higher. When prices fall, the opposite happens. Bids go to a lower price, and asks go lower as well. Level II shows this information through bid and ask columns sorted both according to price—with the highest bid at the top of the bid column and the lowest ask at the top of the ask column, followed by next closest in order—and by the order in which the bids were received. Colors help with the sorting system too.

Market makers are represented by four-letter symbols in the bid-ask columns. Seeing their bids and asks can help you figure out the market makers' individual strategies, which in turn can help your chances of profiting. When refreshing quotes (after selling their previous 1000 shares), market makers can leave their bid or ask the same, lower or raise it, or lower one and raise the other. What they do can tell you about their interest in a stock and their perception of where it is going. If a market maker keeps refreshing the price at the inside market, for example, it is active in the stock, and a price movement may be coming. How fast a large block of a stock is sold or bought can be significant too. A quick sale of a big chunk means support for rising prices, whereas a difficult time selling a large chunk means a stock is probably headed down.

It is important when watching the bids and asks on level II to see who is in the inside market and who is changing the highest bids and offers. For example, whether it is a market maker or an ECN can make a difference, as can the size of the order and whether the entity keeps continually buying or selling. Market makers with large amounts of a stock or big orders from institutions will do what is known as *scale out,* or get out of their position gradually, going along with momentum, rather than get out at the top or the bottom of the spread. You should watch for this sign because when market makers (and specialists, for that matter) start to do this, the current top could be close, and there is a good opportunity to profit.

Finally, it is also important to remember that not all participants in a stock are displayed at all times. There will always be undisplayed participants—parties who are ready to trade but are not yet posting. This is a major unseen force watching and waiting to take advantage like you are. Even through level II, you can never know that these undisplayed participants exist until they actually make a move.

TEENIES

The last key trading concept this chapter will cover is *teenies,* or tiny $\frac{1}{16}$ movements in price. Teenies make it possible to profit from a stock that does not fluctuate by more than small fractional amounts all day long. How do you make money from teenies? By trading several thousand shares at a time. In order to profit from a $\frac{1}{16}$ fluctuation in a stock, you need to trade at least 2000 shares at a time so as to come out ahead before commissions. Brokerage firms do this all the time, because teenies can add up. They also present a much better chance of profit than do fluctuations on a couple hundred shares of a more volatile stock. You can make a living through teenies.

When you make money through a teenie, you are dong it on the spread. This is so because you buy on the bid and sell on the ask, and most stocks do not have bid-ask spreads wider than $\frac{1}{16}$. And as mentioned, you actually should avoid volatile stocks when trying to profit from teenies. You do not want to risk losing more than $\frac{1}{16}$ on a trade because that is all you are aiming to make in the first place.

SUMMARY

When many new traders start, the world of symbols and terms can be very confusing. With so much information flashing across the screen, it can be a bit confusing (and initially overwhelming) to be able to decipher the data. As you will quickly learn, however, the world of symbols and terms is not that confusing after all. The key once again is deciding what information you need to make your trading decisions. Because speed once again is a key weapon for the direct access trader, you want to do everything you can in order to give yourself an edge. Symbols especially happen to be one of the best ways to cram more information on your computer screen, and often many traders only know stocks by their symbols. Direct access traders do not want to waste time having to flip between screens to try to find their information. Everything that can be abbreviated for traders is abbreviated; therefore, it pays to spend some time in getting to know the basics. This is especially where spending some time on a simulation program can be a lot of help. After you spend some time getting familiar with the basic symbols, trading becomes much easier. As for terms, traders have a very different lingo that it helps to become comfortable with. Terms such as *scalping, head and shoulders, hitting the bid,* and others can take a while to become familiar with. Once again, just realize that these are "fancy names" for things that have mostly always existed. Direct access traders are coming up with new lingo every day. The ones that you really need to get familiar with from the beginning are the basics that make direct access trading possible. These include the following:

All or none   An order to purchase or sell a security in which the broker/ dealer is instructed to fill the entire order or not to fill it at all.

Ask price   The price at which market participants offer to sell a security.

Bounce   A redirection in the market that occurs when there is a serious down movement followed by a serious upswing.

Covering the position   Closing a position by buying back the stock that a trader sold short.

Day order   An order that is specified to be filled within the day it is placed or else canceled.

Day trader   A trader who closes out all positions at the end of the day for cash.

Downbid   A decrease of one level in the price of a stock on the Nasdaq.

ECN   Electronic communication network. Investors presented on bid and offer of stock who purchase and sell the stocks in which they are trading.

ECNs sometimes represent market makers, but they are not subjected to SOES. They only accept preference orders.

High bid   When a market maker or ECN wants to pay higher for a stock than anyone else and increases the current bid price. The high bid is the act of increasing the bid price.

Limit order   An order to be filled only at a price no worse than a specified price level, called the *limit price.*

Marker maker   A market participant responsible for providing liquidity, i.e., who stands ready to buy or sell from traders.

Offer   The price at which a market maker offers to sell a stock.

Preference order   Order to buy or sell that is only entered to and seen by a specific market maker or ECN and is not open for anyone else to see or to execute.

Resistance   A price level that represents a psychological barrier for the market, beyond which the price of a stock cannot rise. Often, when a stock reaches the resistance level, investors fear that the price will fall, as it has before, and sell, which causes the price to fall.

SOES   Small Order Execution System. Trading system that allows investors to purchase and sell stocks immediately after they enter an order. The number one benefit is immediate executions.

Specialist   The individual who is in charge of making markets and providing liquidity for stocks traded on the New York Stock Exchange.

Spread   The difference between the bid price and the ask price.

Support   A price level that represents a psychological barrier for the market, beyond which the price of a stock cannot fall. Often, when a stock reaches the support level, investors assume that the price will increase, as it has before, and buy, which causes the price to increase.

Swing   A sudden and dramatic redirection of the market.

Therefore, it just takes some time to get familiar with the new lingo before you will be just as familiar with it as everyone else. In the world of direct access trading, there are so many symbols and terms that no one individual knows them all. Each trader has a little collection that he or she uses and refers to on a consistent basis based on his or her trading style and portfolio. Once you get to know the terms listed above, you can spend more time mastering the others.

QUESTIONS TO ASK YOURSELF

1   How familiar am I with the direct access trading lingo?
2   What are the symbols of the main stocks I plan on trading?
3   How familiar am I with the acronyms used by the different market makers?
4   How familiar am I with the acronyms used by the major ECNs?

C H A P T E R

5

NEWS AND RESEARCH SOURCES

This chapter has two parts. The first will orient you to the different pieces of information and techniques used to determine the state of the market. The second will focus on specific news and research sources that can help you make informed trading decisions.

UNDERSTANDING THE MARKET

General Health of the Economy

One of the most basic but most important clues to the state of the market is the overall health of the U.S. economy. This is so because the overall health of the economy in turn affects the valuation of stocks.

Broad economic indicators that are reported by the Federal Reserve and various government agencies weekly, monthly, and quarterly include, among many others, the following: nonfarm payrolls and unemployment rate, producer and price indices, gross domestic product, retail sales report, durable goods orders report, industrial production report, capacity utilization report, consumer confidence index, and housing starts and building permits. Different indicators are more sensitive to and predictive of the market at different times, and different people interpret the individual indicators in different ways. Nonetheless, if you do not have a basic grasp of economic concepts and how these indicators fit into the overall picture of the economy, you will want to brush up before even thinking about trading actively.

Generally speaking, if the monetary policy of a government allows for controlled expansion, investor sentiment is good, and the market will rise, resulting in a bull market. However, in such a situation, the government needs to be careful that growth does not get out of control. This is where the Federal Reserve (the Fed) comes in: It is the job of the Fed to stimulate controlled expansion and make adjustments in economic policy according to how the economy reacts.

Economic events and policies are not the only factors that affect the markets, however. Both social and political events can have ramifications as well. The most widely accepted reason for this is the fact that, in general, people fear the unknown. When there is social or political uncertainty, the tendency is to transfer monetary holdings into cash.

Finally, there is inflation, an important factor in any economy. Basically, when the economy heats up, prices rise because of an increase in the supply and demand of goods. This means each dollar is worth less. Inflation is therefore another important issue the Fed takes into consideration when adjusting economic policy.

Supply and Demand

The simple law of supply and demand is the key to how the markets work (as well as the key to each individual trading day). Essentially, the market is a constant battle between buyers and sellers. Its direction is a clear result of the volume of buy versus sell orders.

The participation of sellers and buyers at a certain price at a given time, in reaction to various forces that affect the market or an individual stock, is known as *price action*. For long-term investors, short-term fluctuations in price action are not particularly important. For very active traders, however, moment-to-moment supply and demand and the resulting price action are much more significant.

Therefore, the first thing an active trader should do every day is to assess the sentiment and direction of the market at its open. The term *market sentiment* refers to all the good and bad news about all stocks in the market taken together, which will determine which way the market leans. If you can predict which way the market will go, it will help you make successful trades, because orders from the public tend to follow this general sentiment. The important thing is to think ahead of the public, factoring in all the hype about a certain stock or the market as a whole.

If you watch the market from the very beginning, not only will you see how people react to headlines and other news, but you also will start to notice how like stocks have a tendency to move together (unless there is dramatic news about one of them), how big news affects smaller stocks in the same sector, and other patterns. Larger stocks tend to trend with market in general, for example. Stocks within the same sector tend to move in the same direction at the same time. Thus, watching market leaders (large-cap stocks) in individual sectors is very helpful because they often lead the entire sector, and individual sectors in the market often go in different directions. Huge stocks like Microsoft can single-handedly cause huge movements within their entire sector.

Then, as the day goes on, you will need to monitor price activity and look at other indicators (to be explained in more detail in just a few paragraphs) for clues that the market is going to change direction or stay the same.

Most trading takes place during the opening (the first 2 to 2 1/2 hours the market is open) and the closing (the last 2 to 2 1/2 hours). These are therefore the most profitable periods of the trading day. Especially during the open—and in the first half hour of the open in particular—trading ranges tend to be at their widest, and intraday trends are often set. It is important to watch the actions of market makers and specialists then, as well as monitor stocks' and markets' highs and lows. During the closing is when the intraday trends set at the opening tend to play out the strongest, partly because of the rush to place orders before the markets close.

When thinking about supply and demand and how it affects the markets, it is important to remember the old adage that fear is stronger than optimism. This means that stocks fall faster than they rise. When stock prices rise, they tend to do so in steps, but when they fall, sell-offs occur quickly. Also, if bids are strong and the market is advancing, over-exuberance can result. And if there is a lack of bids, panic can ensue as people rush to grab the last remaining good bids. These factors point, once again, to the importance of knowing at all times who is dominating the market and the basic emotions that control it.

Market Sentiment Indicators

Many traders use what are known as *market sentiment indicators* to help them understand the market. We will take a quick tour of some of them here.

In learning about any indicators, however, it is important to remember that they are not absolute trading signals to be used in a vacuum but simply clues to future price action. Some traders assign percentages or ratios to market sentiment indicators to tell them when to buy and sell. This is not a wise idea. You are better off merely monitoring directional changes in the indicators for clues to where the market might go next; you need to learn to *interpret* indicators as opposed to letting them dictate your actions.

Market sentiment indicators are best used in conjunction with the way the market is already trending. For example, if the market is moving in one direction but a favorite indicator says a reversal is coming, it is best to wait until the reversal starts before taking a position. Other times, indicators that are helpful include when the market is showing no trend; in these situations, indicators can help to alert you in which direction the market will move once it starts trending again. In a nutshell: The action of the market always should take precedence over indicators, which should be used only to alert you of possible changes.

This said, here are some of the most common market sentiment indicators used by active traders, in no particular order:

> *Public/specialist short sales data.* This is the number of short sales made by the public divided by the number of short sales made by market makers and specialists over a given period of time. Before the mid-1990s, the public did not often short in greater amounts than specialists and market makers. (In fact, because specialists and market makers often have to short in order to match buy and sell orders, this was considered a professional activity.) But starting in the mid-1990s, there were a number of times when the public shorted above the specialists and market markers after a period of rising prices, and this indicated that market the would continue to rise. However, the public shorting above specialists and market

makers has been such a regular occurrence since then that it is no longer considered such an excellent predictor.

Chicago Board of Exchange (CBOE) put/call ratio. This is the ratio of total puts to total calls over a period of time. Besides for the general market, this ratio is also used for equity options, index options, and individual index options. Because of the growth in trading options and futures, many traders now look at this instead of public/specialist short sales ratios.

A call option gives its owner the right to buy stock at a certain price within a certain time frame. Those who buy call options are bullish, hoping for a rise in prices. A put option gives its owners the right to sell stock at a certain price within a given time frame. Those who buy put options are bearish, hoping for a decline in prices and to make money that way. The higher the number of puts traded versus calls, the higher is the possibility that the stock market is at a low. Therefore, put/call ratios reveal extremes in sentiment.

One of the most common ways to interpret the CBOE put/call ratio is that ratios over 0.80 are bullish and ratios below 0.40 are bearish. Another interpretation is that in bull markets, 4 days of readings greater than 0.50 for the equity-only ratio usually precedes a market rally of at least 5 percent.

High/low logic indicator. This indicator was invented by Norman Fosback in 1979 and was explained in his book *Stock Market Logic* and in his newsletter of the same name. The high/low logic indicator is the lesser of either new highs or new lows in the market as a percentage of total issues traded. It can be calculated either daily or weekly.

The theory behind this indicator is that when a large number of stocks makes both new highs and new lows in the same week, it is a sign of internal weakness in the market. Although this can be a very telling indicator, it is important to remember that tax selling in December can skew new highs and lows. (Some people even suggest ignoring the buy and especially sell signals in from the high/low logic index in December and January.

Advance/decline line. To get this indicator, take the difference between the daily number of advancing issues and the number of declining issues (ignore unchanged issues). Then either add or subtract this figure to or from the cumulative number of issues, depending on what you are looking for. The result is a very basic indicator of the market's overall health.

Lots of rules and systems have been designed around the advance line, but some basic principles are that when the Dow declines while the line is rising, the market will rise. When the Dow advances while the line is falling, market will decline. And when the Dow approaches its previous low and the line is much above where it was at the time of its previous low, the tendency is to be bullish. When the Dow approaches its previous high and the line is much below its previous high, the tendency is to be bearish.

Dow Jones Utilities Average. Most of the time, an extreme upward or downward trend in the utilities average will be followed by a similar trend in the market at large (although it can take a few months for this mirroring effect to occur).

Technical Indicators

The other types of indicators are *technical indicators.* They are the result of something called *technical analysis,* which is the study of volume, price behavior, and various patterns and relationships. Instead of studying a company from the inside, technical analysis looks at it from the outside. It notes how a company's stock has acted in the past and uses charts and graphs to determine where its price is likely to go on a given day.

Many traders believe that at least some of this type of analysis is helpful, if only because so many people use it. Because so many traders are reacting to the same signs, stocks often behave in the predicted way; the basics of technical analysis will create patterns in price just because so many people know about them and act on them. Therefore, it is important to always be thinking ahead about what others will be thinking and how they will be reacting.

Technical analysis is most often contrasted to *fundamental analysis,* which aims to find the true value of a company by trying to understand its internal workings through examining things like its business model, earnings, growth potential, and competition.

In addition to financial factors that help determine if a stock is under- or overvalued, fundamental analysis also considers social, economic, and political factors that may affect the market. Generally speaking, fundamental analysis come into play more and more as an investment time period grows longer.

Probably a good rule of thumb is that investors who plan to buy and hold or make intermediate-term (not intraday) trades are better off using fundamental analysis, but day and other active traders should be familiar with and use technical analysis to understand short-term price action. All investors, however, should combine technical and fundamental analyses in order to best interpret the market. And, of course, any individual indicator should be cross-referenced with both other technical indicators and market sentiment indicators before it is used to make a trading decision.

Some popular technical terms and indicators include

Trends. This is probably the most basic technical term to understand. Trends simply refer to when a stock is moving in one direction, either up or down. An upward trend is a series of price cycles that shows a succession of both higher highs and higher lows. A downward trend is series of price cycles that shows both lower lows and lower highs. More than one trend can be going on at the same time, so it is important to know what time period you are looking at. Weekly, monthly, daily, and even intraday trends can all exist.

Volume. Like the bid, ask, and order size, volume is part of a basic stock quote. Basically, it is the total number of shares—either of a specific stock or of the market as a whole—that have been traded on a given day since the opening. Volume can confirm trends by telling you how interested other people are in a stock. For example, very little volume indicates very little interest (which results in poor liquidity). When the volume of a stock starts to decline, the price usually starts to decline too. In contrast, a rising price with increasing volume normally reflects a stock that is on an uptrend. Level II systems make it possible to sort stocks by volume, and if you notice a stock has moved up a lot on the list, you may want to pay attention to it.

Interpreting volume is not that simple, however. The more volume during a price move, the more significant it is. Low volume may indicate uncertainty or even a reversal, as can falling volume on a rising trend. Heavy volume on breakouts and breakdowns (to be explained in just a few paragraphs) can mean a further trend in that direction. Extremely high volume also can mean high volatility, and trading during high volatility means that you could be caught at the bad end of a rapidly changing price.

Moving averages (MA). These are price averages for a stock over various lengths of time. There are 10- , 20- , 50- , and 200-day moving averages. Each is gotten by averaging a stock's closing prices over the specified period of time. Moving averages are used to confirm trends. A rising MA confirms an upward trend, and a declining one confirms a downward trend. Also, when a stock's price nears a certain, significant MA, sometimes its future movement can be predicted. For example, when a rising stock approaches an important declining MA, it is likely to find some resistance (a point at which its price probably will not go higher).

S&P500 futures. Futures contracts are traded on the floors of Chicago Mercantile Exchange and are probably the most watched indicator for day traders. This is so because a number of large-cap stocks have almost identical intraday price actions to those of certain Standard & Poors (S&P) contracts. Even though fundamentals govern the long-term price action of future contracts, just as for any other kind of commodity, their short-term behavior is often predictive. For example, since it is usually thought that future stock prices will be higher than those today, contracts selling at a discount is a bearish sign.

Support and resistance. The *support level* is the price area at which a stock has more buyers than sellers and historically has found a hard time moving lower because there are enough buyers to prevent a further decrease in price. Conversely, the *resistance level* is the price area at which a stock has more sellers than buyers and historically has had a hard time going higher because there are enough sellers to prevent a further increase in price. Another term for resistance is *ceiling*.

Support and resistance can be found daily, weekly, or even intraday. When examining intraday support and resistance, it is important to note not only the highs and lows of yesterday and today, yesterday's closing price, and today's open but also past support and resistance levels and those from earlier in the day.

It is also important to remember that support and resistance are areas rather than exact prices. If a stock is heading toward a clear resistance level and there is heavy selling before it gets there, with parties coming in and trading early, this is a sign of weakness and is called *overshooting. Undershooting,* in contrast, is a sign of strength and occurs when people come in and buy before the obvious support level. This shows their desire for a stock and their willingness to compete for it.

Breakouts and breakdowns. A *breakout* occurs when a stock has broken a former resistance level and seeks to find a new one. Because it has been shown that parties are willing to pay even more for the stock, additional buyers are attracted, and the stock moves toward an even higher resistance level. The old resistance level becomes the new support level. In contrast, a breakdown occurs when the old support area becomes the new resistance area because prices have dropped below the original support. Prices then move to find a new, lower support level.

Some breakouts and breakdowns are false alarms, however. For example, a sign of a true breakout is when the price comes back down to the first resistance level and there are enough buyers there. In this case, the upward trend will continue. However, if there are not enough buyers there, then the breakout is not real, and the stock will move downward when this fact has been exposed. Therefore, when looking at breakouts and breakdowns, it is very important to see if the former support or resistance level has been tested.

Gaps. These occur when a stock opens at a price higher than its previous day's high or lower than its previous day's low. A series of price levels has been skipped because of some kind of change in sentiment. News announcements, often having to do with earnings, and analyst up- or downgrades are some causes of gaps. Gaps also can happen as a result of developments in the overall market between the close of one day and the opening of the next.

Gaps happen almost daily and almost always attract trading, usually in the direction of the gap. The bigger the gap, the more activity will occur, and the greater the effect it will have on the market. Gaps of 3/8 or less are generally not considered significant.

Breakaway and exhaustion gaps are two common types of gaps. *Breakaway gaps* are gaps in which the price of a stock opens above the former resistance level or below the former support. *Exhaustion gaps* occur when a breakaway gap fails and there is a retrenchment. Both these types of gaps are usually due to big news, and it is generally not a good idea to trade against them.

Overbought/oversold. These indicators are very simple. A stock that has been bought, usually during a rally, at prices too high to be sustained is *overbought.* A decline in price may be coming. A stock that, during a sell-off, has been sold at prices too low to be sustained is *oversold.* A rise in price may be coming.

Volatility. A stock's volatility can be determined by its degree of price fluctuation. For day traders, a stock that moves only within a $1 range during a time period of a week or so is usually not volatile enough to profit from. But a stock that moves up and down $1 within a few minutes is usually too volatile. A stock that moves within a $1 range on a daily basis is usually about right.

Another method of picking stocks whose volatility is good is to check each morning for stocks that are up or down at least 10 percent from the day before. This usually means that there has been news of some kind to profit from.

Cautionary note: Anyone who is trading highly volatile stocks probably should not hold them overnight. This is so because these stocks are the most likely to gap down the next morning.

Daily, Weekly, and Seasonal Patterns

Technical analysis also looks closely at all kinds of patterns. Some of them are listed below. Again, remember that you should never base your trading decisions completely on any one of these patterns. If you enter the market based on certain expectations and it does not act the way you anticipated, you should adjust accordingly.

Momentum patterns. Momentum is the buying or selling pressure that keeps prices moving in one direction until pressure in the opposite direction causes a reversal. High volume and volatility can keep momentum going in one direction. Momentum can shift day to day as well as intraday, but these fluctuations do not necessarily change the long-term direction of the stock. Extreme momentum days are days of unusual price action that has not been seen for the past few months. An extreme momentum day usually signifies a continuation of momentum in that direction for the next few days.

V-bottom reversals. These tend to happen intraday. They occur when the Dow has been negative the entire season, is down at least 0.75 percent on the day, and suddenly makes a furious comeback. Similar to this is the *late-day upside surge pattern.* This normally happens during the last 2 to 2½ hours of a day that has seen trendless and/or slightly up and down price action. Like the V-bottom reversal, it is only significant when it comes after a down day or a period of falling prices.

Best percentage days. Many people believe that Mondays are weak days in the market and that Fridays are the best days. The numbers do show that historically this has been the case. However, in the 1990s, Mondays were the best day of the week to push the long side of a stock; in fact, one statistic says that 70 percent of the Dow's gain through the mid-1990s occurred on Mondays. This just shows that you need to be flexible. Take advantage of patterns as much as possible while they are happening, and adjust when they become less effective.

One percent true selling day. This type of pattern is indicated by the Dow, the S&P500, the Nasdaq 100, and the Russell 200 all closing down 1 percent or more on the same trading day after at least 2 weeks of rising prices. A 1 percent true selling day can be predictive of a serious price decline on the way.

Friday-to-Monday pattern. Better than average strength in a stock on Friday is likely to be followed by more strength on Monday. Weak action on Friday is likely to be followed by more weak action on Monday. When this pattern is broken, it is usually indicative of a short-term trend change.

Monthly pattern. According to research by Norman Fosback and Arthur Merril, the stock market has a bullish bias during first the 4 and the last trading day of every month. This bias also has been demonstrated on the 2 days preceding any market holiday. (These include Christmas, New Year's Day, President's Day, Good Friday, Memorial Day, Fourth of July, and Labor Day.) Also according to this research, the 1½-month period starting 2 days before Thanksgiving and ending with the fifth day in January accounts for 40 percent of the stock market's entire price returns over the past 70 years. Even though lots of people know about the year-end rally, it is a pattern that has held up over time (unlike many other patterns, which can start to diminish once people pick up on them). Clearly, this suggests that you might consider taking greater risks during this year-end period.

End-of-quarter bias. In the last few years of the 1990s, it was not good to be in the Dow and large-cap stocks on the last trading day of each quarter (in March, June, September, and December). Russell 200 and small-cap stocks, however, showed gains on these days. Since large caps usually reverse their decline in the first few days of a new quarter, you may want to exit small caps at the very end of the last trading day and get back into large caps for the beginning of next quarter. However, this is one of those patterns which is becoming well known and may start to diminish.

January barometer. Another school of thought is that the market's performance in January is a predictor of how the rest of the year will be. A man by the name of Victor Neiderhoffer tested the Dow Jones Industrials from 1935 to 1995 and found that in the years when the Dow declined in January, it closed down for the rest of the year half the time. In those years when the Dow rose in January, it closed up for the year 80 percent of the time.

Presidential cycle. In general, the third year of a president's term usually sees the best performance of stock prices. The next-best year is the fourth; then comes the second and the first.

Decennial cycle. This theory holds that there is bias in stock performances depending on last digit of the year. Since 1880, the S&P500 Index has never had a down year in years ending in the number 5. The worst years have been those ending in 7.

The Federal Reserve. All traders go by the rule that you should never fight the market's momentum or the Federal Reserve. This is so because, in the short term, interest rates are the main driver of the stock market, and the Fed controls interest rates. It does this in a number of ways, including through discount rates, the Fed Funds rate, bank reserve requirements, and stock margin requirements (although the last two are not used that frequently anymore). Some analysis has found that the S&P500 usually increases in the months following discount rate reductions (and the increase is even more dramatic following two consecutive rate cuts). Also, the Fed decreasing the Fed Fund rates historically has been very good for the market.

RESEARCH SOURCES

Because of new technologies, individual investors now have a level playing field with professional traders. Lower costs and high-speed direct access give individual investors the ability to send orders extremely quickly and for very little money. Favorable Securities and Exchange Commission (SEC) and National Association of Securities Dealers (NASD) regulations make more sources of information available. All this gives individual investors the ability to make huge profits. However, as always, there is still competition for those profits. Investors new to direct access trading need knowledge and skills, not just tools.

The big difference between professionals and beginners is experience. So how do you compensate for this? Through education. You must learn as much as you can about the markets. One way of doing this is to examine all your past trades. You should always reconstruct all your trading decisions and learn from your mistakes by figuring out where and why you went wrong. Dissecting your trades carefully can help you to find clues to your successes and failures.

Another way of learning about the markets is to read everything you can get your hands on: magazines, newspapers, newsletters, Web sites, and more. However, information overload can make it difficult to sort through the information and determine which of it is good. Just remember to use your common sense and learn to filter data instead of believing everything you read. Also, always cross-reference any information with other sources.

News

Many short-term traders use the instant and constant availability of news to profit by taking positions based on its information before the majority of investors have heard it. Types of news items that can be used in this way include stock splits, lawsuits, and mergers, all of which can greatly affect a stock's price action intraday.

You definitely do not have to read every single newspaper and watch every single TV show about the market each day. This can be overload and will not necessarily help you in your trades. However, you should be aware of general market news and indicators and watch the opening and early hours of the market to get a sense of its flow. Again, do not watch or read any major news sources to actually get the information but rather to know what the market will be reacting to—and to interpret and anticipate those responses. Here are some key sources that can help you keep current:

CNBC. CNBC is the leader in providing constant, up-to-date information, including news and more detailed stories on the markets, as well as interviews with people about rumors, events, breaking news, and announcements that can affect stock prices. Active traders should have it on all day long and realize that its news and coverage will affect the supply and demand of stocks. The adage "Buy on rumor, sell on news" still holds true. CNBC's shows with news and commentary begin at 5 A.M. and end at 7:30 P.M. "CNBC After Hours" can be helpful too.

Bloomberg TV. This is another cable channel that offers real-market information and discussion of today's markets and its headlines. You can use it to help you monitor the market, although you must learn to interpret its recommendations or opinions differently depending on whether you are a day trader or more intermediate-term investor.

Television

Television news offers a surprising number of finance-related programs that may be of interest to traders, particularly new traders who are just beginning to familiarize themselves with the inner workings of markets and stocks. Many of these programs feature market and product analysis and highlight current financial events that may be of interest to investors. Some traders enjoy listening and watching to financial news as they trade, but many others find that there are other sources that deliver faster information, such as Web sites. Still others find that a television may make it more difficult for them to concentrate on trading. Regardless, there are many programs that are not on during trading hours, and these often can offer a wider perspective on the economy, which can be good after a day of trading only several stocks. Many traders find these programs to be interesting and helpful.

CNN

The giant of television news, CNN offers a wide variety of financial programming:

"Ahead of the Curve"
(Monday–Friday, 5:00–7:00 A.M. *ET).*

This program opens the financial news coverage of the day with a look at both international and U.S. markets, including a constantly updated review of stock, bond, currency, and commodity exchange results from around the world. The show also takes a second look at the top financial stories from the previous day and predicts the impact they will have on the current day's market. This show may be particularly interesting for traders who trade international assets.

"Street Sweep"
(Monday–Friday, 3:59–4:30 P.M. *ET).*

Anchored live from CNN's classy studio overlooking the New York Stock Exchange trading floor, this program begins as soon as the trading day ends. The program strives to provide an immediate and general recap of the day's market performance, as well as recent market and corporate news. The show often features guests, ranging from CEOs to brokers and market analysts, who assess the trading day and offer their predictions for the rest of the week. Since this program airs during the time that many online traders are reviewing their gains and losses, it may not be a bad idea to tune in while you analyze your day. For newcomers to the trading world, this program may be helpful to give you an overview of how your stocks relate to the market as a whole.

"Moneyline News Hour"
(weekdays, 6:30 and 11:30 P.M. ET).

This show covers each day's business and financial news. Reports range from company performance and developments to stocks and bonds. It also reviews business as it related to politics, international events, entertainment, and sports. The show does offer traders some information, such as news on the Federal Reserve, that is not found on other financial news programs. It is usually a good review of the day's business news.

"Your Money"
(Monday, 10:30 P.M. ET, Saturday, 7:00 A.M. ET, Sunday 2:30 A.M. ET).

This program prides itself on featuring in-depth financial analysis "with plain-speaking, jargon-free coverage." The show highlights general investment trends and gives tips on how to manage money. Topics covered include savings, investments, real estate, credit, and taxes. The show is not dedicated solely to stocks, and those who have been trading for some time will find that it rarely addresses topics to help them trade better. As indicated by the times at which the program airs, it will not be releasing crucial market information that could give a trader a needed advantage. The show is best meant for those who are still learning the basic concepts in finance and money management.

"Moneyweek"
(Friday, 10:30 P.M. ET, Saturday 3:00 P.M. ET, Sunday, 12:30 A.M. ET).

This program is the weekend edition of "Moneyline," CNN's weekday financial news hour. The show tries to provide an overview of the week's financial activity and often focuses on weekly stock performance. It also looks internationally, frequently calling on correspondents looking at the markets in London and Tokyo. The show is geared toward individuals who do not follow the market closely, often straying away from pure statistics to analyze what the market's activity means for consumers.

"Business Unusual"
(weeknights, 8:30 P.M. ET, Tuesday 10:30 P.M. ET, Sunday 6:30 P.M. ET).

This program takes a stab at "the new economy" and looks closely at what companies are doing to create new products and to survive in the global marketplace. If often looks at Internet companies, and examines the new technologies they are using to get ahead. It attempts to show consumers and business owners how new ideas are changing the way the economy works. While traders may find some of the stories interesting, the show is very feature-oriented, and not as valuable to those who want hard-core technical information.

CNBC

CNBC prides itself as being the financial news station that corporate officials, traders, and investors use most often. The station features around-the-clock financial news. Some of the more beneficial and popular programs are described below.

"Today's Business"
(weekdays, 5:00–7:00 A.M. *ET).*

This program offers an introduction to the day's market, analyzing events of the previous day and offering predictions. It also gives an international perspective, showing live action from trading floors in Europe and Asia and discussing the impact that foreign markets may have on the U.S. stock market during the trading day. It also has an enjoyable segment called "Breakfast with a CEO," as well as a "Stock Pickers Club."

"Squawk Box"
(weekdays, 7:00–10:00 A.M. *ET).*

This program tries to get viewers the insider perspective from the trading floor and investment banks. It attempts to track strategies and interviews Wall Street professionals prior to the opening of the market. Traders may want to keep this show on as they prepare for trading to begin.

"Power Lunch"
(weekdays, 12:00–2:00 P.M. *ET).*

This show gets a good deal of its programming from viewers; phone calls and emails are answered live on the show. The show also looks at companies and topics that are not yet in the mainstream in its "By Request" segment. These are companies that may be of interest to viewers but are currently not widely known.

"Market Wrap"
(weekdays, 4:00–6:00 P.M. *ET).*

This program begins as soon as the trading day is over and offers comprehensive analysis of the day's market events and what it means for investors. The show is also well known for its weekly special events. On Friday, anchor Bill Griffeth leads a roundtable conversation on the current events of the business week, featuring Bill Wolman, chief economist at *Business Week,* and Larry Ludlow, chief economist at American Skandia. Another popular feature is "The Internet Investor," a segment that covers investing in Internet companies. There are also frequent specials on day trading.

"Business Center"
(weekdays, 6:30–8:30 P.M. *ET).*

Broadcast live from the New York Stock Exchange (NYSE), this program provides a summary and overview of the day's business and financial news. A segment called "Trader Talk" may be of interest to many traders. In this segment, traders are interviewed on the NYSE floor. It may be very helpful for those who trade at home to hear these traders' perspective on the day's market activity.

BLOOMBERG

The financial media superpower Bloomberg offers a wide variety of detailed television programming that is available from DirecTV and on cable systems. It is also available on the USA Network on weekdays from 5:00 to 8:00 A.M. ET and on Saturdays from 5:30 to 7:00 A.M.

Bloomberg is intense, offering news and analysis 24 hours a day, Monday to Friday. Weekends offer general financial news. The schedule for an average day is as follows:

5:00 A.M. to 12:00 P.M. ET.

Beginning with predictions about the market and recapping stories from the previous day, the news coverage continues with reports on stocks, mergers and acquisitions, and money flow, as well as futures, bonds, Web stocks, and the Nasdaq. The opening bell is covered at 9:00 A.M., and morning trends are reviewed.

"Box Lunch"
(12:00–1:00 P.M. ET).

This program looks ahead to the rest of the afternoon market activity and reviews what has occurred in the markets during the morning. Guests are often brought in to analyze the day's events.

1:00 to 8:00 P.M. ET.

Covering the market in the afternoon and the closing of the market, the coverage summarizes the day's major stories and offers predictions for where the market might head in the next few days. It also covers market moving after the bell, a subject that is often not reported as immediately on other networks.

8:00 P.M. to 5:00 A.M. ET.

Bloomberg never stops reporting; the red-eye news coverage mostly includes news on foreign markets that are already up and running. Special reports are given from the Tokyo and London Bloomberg bureaus.

Bloomberg also features several daily special reports that usually last only several minutes. These are generally more focused features, which often address strategy for buying and selling stocks. Two of these special reports are described below:

"Money Flow"
(weekdays, 5:39, 7:24, and 10:47 A.M. ET).

Money flow is the amount of money that is going in and out of a stock; a stock price can drop even as its money flow increases. This program analyzes money flow in comparison with stock prices and makes suggestions about stock purchases of over 10,000 shares by examining key divergences, when, for example, money is flowing out of a stock even as its price increases. The show is a good way for traders to examine a particular trading technique and may be valuable for new traders who are still trying to determine their own strategies.

"Web Watch"
(weekdays, 6:25 and 9:55 A.M. ET).

This program looks closely at Internet stocks and advises investors on what types of companies will be successful. It also examines the risks of investing with Internet stocks and the differences between these stocks and others.

Print Publications

Investors Business Daily (IBD). This publication has what is considered the best, most current coverage of news that affects the markets. There is lots of good material here, including sections on companies in the news, stocks with the greatest percentage rise in volume, stocks with the highest percentage rise in price, stocks in the news charts, and general market indicators.

The Wall Street Journal. A must-read for financial and other news.

Barron's. This newspaper is good for recaps of the week. Its "Market Laboratory" section has data on the total weekly trading activity of specialists, the public, and NYSE members, which is compiled by the SEC with a 2-week lag. Like *Business Week, Barron's* is a publication that the general public tends to read on weekends, so the articles in it can affect the following few trading days. It is good to know what is inside so you can anticipate whether the contents will affect the market.

Magazines. Popular magazines include *Business Week, Money, Bloomberg Personal Finance, Worth, Forbes, Mutual Funds, AAII Journal, Smart Money,* and *Technical Analysis of Stocks and Commodities.*

Newsletters. Market Logic, The Chartist, Investor's Digest, Hulbert Financial Digest, MoniResearch, and *Commodity Traders Consumer Reports* are some of the most useful newsletters.

Market Sentiment Polls

Various polling services exist to try to measure market sentiment to find out about extremes of optimism or pessimism. Various different kinds of investors are polled: brokers, advisors, newsletter writers, the public, and others. The theory is that when an opinion of some kind becomes too extreme, a reversal is coming (because the market has run out of new buyers and sellers.) Some of the most popular sentiment services are listed below:

> *Investors Intelligence.* This is the oldest of the services. It takes a weekly poll of over 130 investment advisory services and breaks down the data into percentages of bulls, bears, and those who are bullish but expecting a correction. Investors Intelligence is available every Wednesday at 11 A.M. EST through a pay-per-call number and is also usually on CNBC between 11 and 12.
>
> *Market Vane.* Market Vane conducts polls that are geared more toward short-term traders. The sentiment numbers Market Vane gives are for stock index futures, and thus they fluctuate more quickly than those in Investors Intelligence. Market Vane has a daily hotline that can be accessed after 5 P.M. Pacific Time through a pay-per-call number.
>
> *Consensus.* This service is very similar to Market Vane. Its numbers are available Tuesday mornings through a pay-per-call number.

Market Vane also has a newsletter that features a weekly poll of trading recommendations from over 100 market letter writers and trading firms specializing in futures. The consensus of these recommendations, called the *Bull's Consensus Index,* goes from 0 to 100 percent. The higher the number, the more bullish it is.

Interestingly, Earl Hadady, author of the book *Contrary Opinion,* says that conventional wisdom is almost always wrong as far as trading goes. Thus he believes that "safe" consensus numbers tend to stay within 30 to 70 percent. But when almost everyone is bullish and that number is higher, the market almost always declines, he says. Conversely, when almost everyone is bearish, the market almost always rallies.

Therefore, one common interpretation of the Bull's Consensus Index is that at 30 percent, an oversold condition is developing; at 70 percent, an overbought condition is developing. And as the numbers approach the extremes of 0 and 100 percent, a reversal is coming. According to this view, you should not buy when consensus is in extremes of bullishness or sell when it is in extremes of bearishness. This shows once again why, although you should be aware of current news or opinions expressed in magazines, newspapers, and other media, you should not make trading decisions based on them.

Data Vendors

A great deal of data is now available for free from a wide variety of Web sites. However, for the trader who needs an even greater supply of data, there are fortunately professional data vendors. These sellers offer the most comprehensive data sets around and package them efficiently to allow users to easily find what they need. Data can be ordered for each trading day, and many traders find it helpful to receive an evening email with nicely organized data from the day's activity. Data vendors usually can organize this type of market data on daily, weekly, and yearly bases. Data are also often available from the middle of the century as well, although this type of data may be less useful to the average trader. Data are usually either downloaded or copied onto a CD-ROM and mailed.

Below are summaries of two data providers; there are several other vendors that may be considered, such as Bonneville Market Information, Data Broadcasting Corp., Dial Data, Prophet Information Services, and Telescan, Inc. Data vendors have different audiences in mind; because all these providers generally offer organized number sets, even the most basic ones are less friendly to the beginning trader. Other data vendors are more geared to market makers rather than individual investors. Traders considering a data service should first make sure that it is a tool that they will actually use and one that will help them. It does not help traders to receive information and never bother to read it. In addition, traders should make sure that they like the way that the data are formatted, because different data formats suit different needs.

Commodity Systems, Inc. (CSI), www.csidata.com. Commodity Systems has been widely regarded as one of the most accurate and efficient data providers. The September 1999 issue of *Futures Magazine* featured a lead story about the accuracy of the top end-of-day data services for investors, and CSI came out on top. The study showed that CSI competitors had an error rate 385 percent higher than that of CSI. Daily data updates are supplied by modem and are also available as compilations on CD-ROM. Historical daily data dating back to the middle of the twentieth century is also available. CSI's historical coverage includes all commodity markets gathered from over 50 futures exchanges; more than 95 percent of the commodities in the inventory extend back to the initial public offering (IPO). CSI also offers daily summary data on all NYSE stocks and many stocks from the American and Nasdaq exchanges. Commodity Systems also offers a wide variety of other data and data management programs. Its Unfair Advantage software delivers sorted and formatted commodity data. Other programs are available to help traders understand and use their data. Fees for daily data begin at $13 per month and, according to CSI, usually do not exceed $40. Corporate users are charged a higher rate. All customers also receive CSI's monthly *Technical Journal*, which includes information on new markets, mergers, and stock splits.

Genesis Financial Data Services, www.gfds.com. Genesis Financial Data Services has been providing financial data since 1983 and offers end-of-the-day information on commodities, stocks, options, and mutual funds, tick by tick information on commodities, and specialty information such as "Public Sentiment." The software is downloadable from their site, via the Internet or through a direct modem connection. Other historical data are also available on request. Genesis offers several data packages. The Standard Navigator is the basic software version offered, and it allows the user to download standard data from the site. It also provides basic graphing utilities. The cost is $95, or it is free with a history order of $200 or more. The Professional Navigator includes all the benefits of the Standard Navigator and also allows users to convert data to multiple formats so that different analysis tools can be used. Cost is $249 or $149 with a history order of more than $200. Other new products in the works include Ultimanager, which is a trading evaluation and money management backtesting software tool.

News Wires and Web Sites

Types of information that can be found online include headlines and commentary, technical and fundamental information, scanning software (software packages that help you to identify specific patterns and do daily market scanning), and training classes and seminars (many of which can be rip-offs). Here are some of the best online resources:

Real-time news wires. These include Bloomberg, Reuters, Dow Jones, and Telerate. All of them provide lots of research and information, and many traders rely primarily on their scrolling data to make trading decisions. However, these services can be very expensive because they require a dedicated news and research terminal.

Yahoo.com. This is a great place to check the foreign markets.

Quicken.com. This is especially good for tracking stocks and the portfolios of your mutual funds.

Dailystocks.com. This allows you to see how different industry groups and indexes are performing intraday.

Marketwatch.com. This provides good summaries after the market closes.

Cme.com. This is the Chicago Mercantile Exchange's site. For those who are interested, you can follow the S&P futures in real time through a tool called Globex.

Decisionpoint.com. This is one of the best Web sites for those who like indicators, charts, and other types of technical analysis.

SUMMARY

With the advent of the Internet, the number of news and research sources has grown exponentially. Once upon time, there were the *Wall Street Journal, Barron's,* your local newspaper, and a couple of good magazines. Today, we have a wave of new print, television, and especially online sources of information for investors. Never before has it been easier to find out information pertaining to your stocks and even having it sent to you automatically. Where your stockbroker used to have all the power because he or she got you good research reports and other so-called special information, the power has been entirely transferred to the individual. What has happened now, however, is that there is a glut of information available to everyone, so once again, the concept of personalization becomes extremely important. The one thing that is constant in the financial world is that everyone likes to put in his or her two cents, and most of the time views differ in some way or another. Therefore, the key is finding trusted sources of information and data feeds on which you feel comfortable basing trading decisions. For direct access traders, CNBC seems to be the one constant that everyone looks at. In fact, there have been times when stocks have been profiled in the morning and traders say they can see the movement of the stock as they are either giving it high marks or downgrading it. This is a good example of what effect a powerful news source such as CNBC or the *Wall Street Journal* can have. It is not that their information is always a 100 percent right or better than anyone else's, but rather that there are so many traders, investors, and other individuals reading these news sources that they tend to have a great deal of influence and credibility in the marketplace.

The other important thing to realize about news and research sources is the way that other individuals react to the same information. What drives individual stock prices is the price at which individuals are willing to buy or sell a particular stock. Therefore, it is important to be able to realize the effect a particular piece of news can have on a stock, just based on the reaction the masses will have to it. A great example is when the Fed declares whether it is going to raise, maintain, or reduce interest rates. The actual act of adjusting the rates does not have an immediate impact, but the reaction to these announcements causes an immediate change in overall market sentiment, which can affect a stock you own in any industry. Therefore, it becomes just as important to understand the effect news can have on other individuals.

Technical analysis, primarily based on charts or graphs, intimidates many new traders. What is important to realize is that there are many ways to use charts and graphs, and even some of the most advanced traders use them only in the simplest of ways. For example, it is very easy to see if a stock is trending upward or is at a new high on a chart. In addition, charts are very helpful in learning about the history of a stock. One of the most valuable lessons is to look at where the stock has moved significantly and go back and find out what news made it move this way. This often can be one of the best sources of information on how to trade a stock the next time a similar event occurs. A bit more advanced is using what is called *support and resistance lines,* which day traders use to determine how a stock is going to move in the next hour or even minute. It shows the up and down movements of a stock and is one of the most widely used methods of analyzing charts by traders. Traders use this information to decide the best time to buy or sell a stock and get in on the best price possible. This book does not get into the advanced functions of technical analysis, but there are plenty of books entirely devoted to specific forms of analysis that you can get into later on. The important thing to realize is that you can learn over time once you get comfortable with the basic indicators.

Another important factor is what type of direct access trader you are going to be. Day traders need predominantly technical information and rely heavily on the use of charts and other forms of technical analysis. They are looking for immediate information that is usually not based on fundamental analysis. In fact, some day traders do not even know the names of the stocks they are trading, only the stock symbols they use to punch the stock up with. However, for longer-term direct access traders, it is very important to get the right combination of fundamental and technical analysis. Relying strictly on either technical or fundamental analysis will give you an inaccurate picture of any extended duration of time. There is never any way to know for certain using either method of analysis, but longer-term direct access traders should look to pick stocks that have good fundamentals as well as technical indicators.

Figures 5–1 through 5–32 are screen shots of a variety of news and research resources for direct access traders. Go to the Web site of the appropriate company for more information.

QUESTIONS TO ASK YOURSELF

1 What information do you like to see before you make a trade?

2 How often do you want to receive news on your stocks?

3 What type of trader are you going to be?

4 Do you plan on using fundamental or technical analysis or a combination of both?

5 How much time do you want to spend analyzing news and research on your stocks on a daily, weekly, and monthly basis?

6 What type of information do you like receiving the best—television, print (newspapers and magazines), or Internet-based?

7 What type of information do you like to receive (analyst reports, breaking news, technical analysis)?

8 How comfortable are you with charts and graphs?

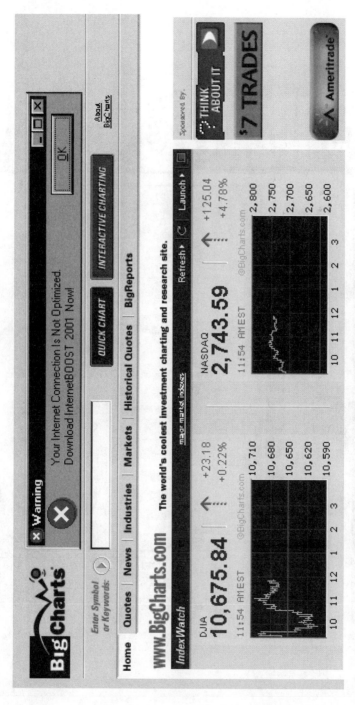

Figure 5-1. Charting a world of investment information. (*Courtesy of BigCharts, www.bigcharts.com.*)

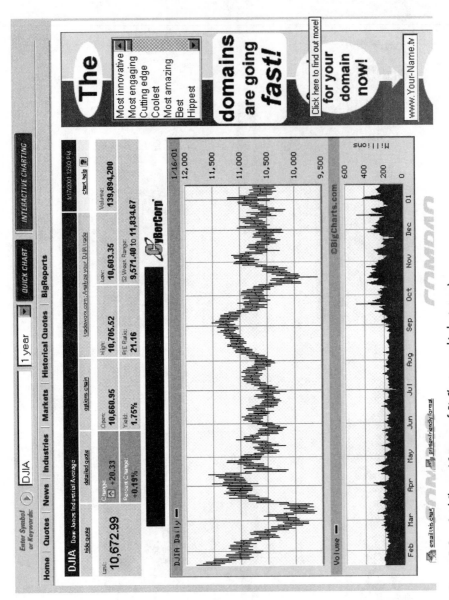

Figure 5-2. QuickCharts. (*Courtesy of BigCharts,* www.bigcharts.com.)

CMGI CMGI Inc. 1/17/2001 12:28 PM

Last:	Change:	Open:	High:	Low:	Volume:
7 13/16	1 1/8	7 17/32	7 15/16	7 1/32	13,357,000
	Percent Change:	Yield:	P/E Ratio:	52 Week Range:	
	16.82%	n/a	n/a	3.625 to 151.50	

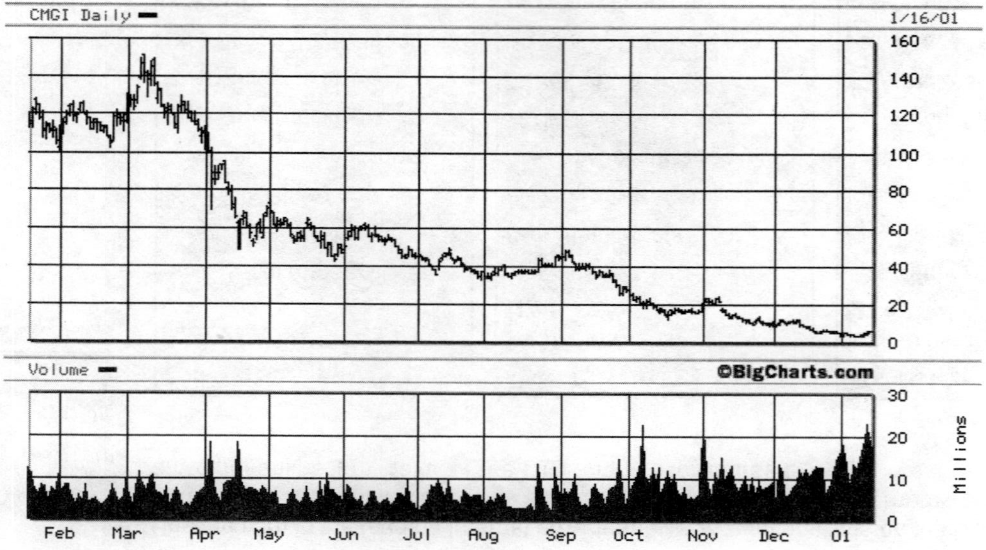

Company Data

Company Name:	CMGI Inc.
Dow Jones Industry:	Industrial Services
Exchange:	NASDAQ NM
Shares Outstanding:	319,311,000

Figure 5-3. Interactive chart for CMG Information Services, Inc. (*Courtesy of BigCharts,* www.bigcharts.com.)

Figure 5-4. Briefing.com home page. (*Courtesy of Briefing.com.*)

Figure 5-5. Briefing.com stock ticker. *(Courtesy of Briefing.com.)*

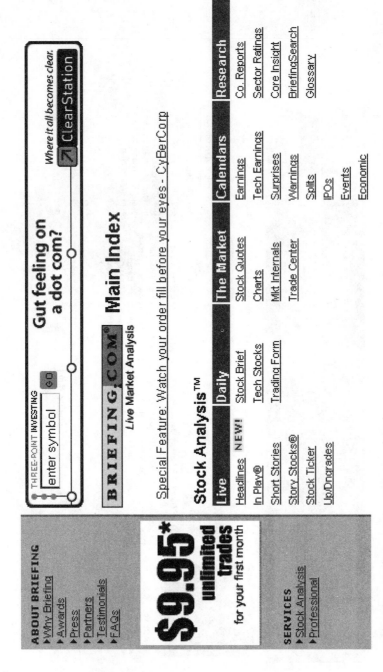

Figure 5-6. Briefing.com index. (*Courtesy of Briefing.com.*)

Figure 5-7. Briefing stock quotes. (*Courtesy of Briefing.com.*)

EDGAR ONLINE
http://www.edgar-online.com

Home

Quick Search: Ticker Symbol ▼ | GO

SEC Filings
- Today's Filings
- This Week's Filings
- Full Search
- Full Text Search
- People

IPO Express
- IPO Headlines
- Latest Pricings
- Upcoming Pricings
- Latest Filings

InsiderTrader

Compensation

FD-Express

Analysis
00110
10100

Electronic | Retrieval

Welcome to *EDGAR Online*.

Throughout the year, every U.S. public company is required to disclose the critical business, financial and competitive details of their activities to the SEC. ***EDGAR Online*** gives the professional and individual user fast and easy access to this SEC information. Register now for our free or subscription services.

Latest Quarterly & Annual Reports

NUOASIS RESORTS INC QUARTERLY REPORT (10QSB)

GEOGRAPHICS INC QUARTERLY REPORT (10-Q)

CASTLE HOLDING CORP ANNUAL REPORT (10KSB)

RADIANT TECHNOLOGY CORP ANNUAL REPORT (10-K)

HARRELL HOSPITALITY GROUP INC ANNUAL REPORT (10KSB)

***EDGAR Online*'s
Questions of the Day**

Next Question
Source: EDGAR Online SEC.nets

Figure 5-8. The source for today's SEC filings. (*Courtesy of EDGAR Online, ©EDGAR Online, Inc.*)

Figure 5-9. Latest filings. (*Courtesy of EDGAR Online, © EDGAR Online, Inc.*)

Figure 5-10. EDGAR Online Personal. (*Courtesy of EDGAR Online,* ©*EDGAR Online, Inc.*)

94

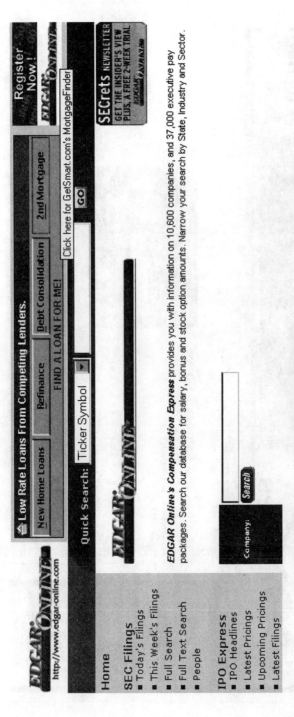

Figure 5-11. Compensation Express. (*Courtesy of EDGAR Online, ©EDGAR Online, Inc.*)

Figure 5-12. IPO Express. *(Courtesy of EDGAR Online, ©EDGAR Online, Inc.)*

Your FREE Book Is Waiting -- Sign up Today!

INVESTORAMA | Home | **Financial Guides** | My Investorama | SHOP | JOIN

Tue, Jan 2, 2001

Community — Tools — Best of the Web — News & Features

● Who's Online Now?

Member Log In · Boards · Groups · Stock PowerSearch

You Are Here: Home -> Financial Guides

Choose Your Financial Guide . . . .
And begin your journey to financial freedom

Stocks
Conservative Investors Enjoy Tech Market Downturn
The value investors who've stuck to their guns over the past several years are finally having their day in the sun.

28,981 Members

Mutual Funds
It May Be Time for an Asset Allocation Fund
If you'd rather do just about *anything* besides re-balance your portfolio, check into asset allocation funds.

Start to Invest
Checklist To Help You Achieve Financial Goals
Get your new year started out right with this to-do list of the essential money moves.

19,154 Members

Retirement Investing
401(k) Choices for Job Changers
It's your future -- don't cash it out.

17,751 Members

Figure 5-13. Investorama home page. (*Courtesy of Investorama.com, www.investorama.com.*)

97

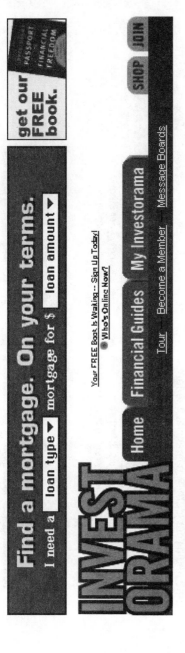

Figure 5-14. Financial guides. (*Courtesy of Investorama.com, www.investorama.com.*)

Figure 5-15. Message board directory. *(Courtesy of Investorama.com, www.investorama.com.)*

Figure 5-16. Silicon Investor home page. (*Used with permission of Go2Net, Inc.; all rights reserved.*)

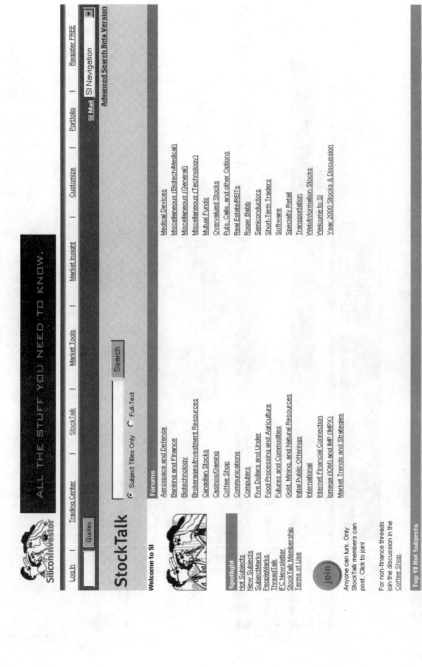

Figure 5-17. Stock talk. (*Used with permission of Go2Net, Inc.; all rights reserved.*)

Log In | Trading Center | StockTalk | Market Tools | Market Insight | Customize | Portfolio | Register FREE

Quotes   SI Mail SI Navigation

Market Tools Menu

Market Tools

Market Monitor
Delivers a quick snapshot of key indices and indicators.

Up/Downgrades
Provides recent changes to key analyst opinions.

Movers & Shakers
Shows you what's hot and what's not.

Bond Market SnapShot
Offers key bond pricing and yield curve.

$ IPOs
Updates you on recent filings, pricings and after-market reports.

Reuters Top News
Informs you with the latest financial, political, sports and entertainment news, and more.

Annual Reports
Free annual reports for over 4,000 companies in North America and Europe.

Figure 5-18. Market Tools menu. (*Used with permission of Go2Net, Inc.; all rights reserved.*)

SiliconInvestor

| Log In | Trading Center | StockTalk | Market Tools | Market Insight | Customize | Portfolio | Register FREE |

| Quotes |

FIND: Enter Request Below

| Best Trading Value | 🔍 SEARCH |

Category: FREE Quotes
FIND ALL Fast Executions
Lower Rates

SI Mail | SI Navigation ▸

Market Insight

Daily Market Rap with Bill Fleckenstein
Air Ball: Revisiting the Bubble Blowoff
Today's Rap is part of a nine-part series of reruns highlighting some of the mania's highest highs, lowest lows and most turbulent twists from January to April 2000.

Threadtalk by David Zgodzinski
2001: An economic odyssey
With a new year and a new U.S. president, investors ponder the alternatives for Alan Greenspan.

IFC with Mark Johnson
Techs to move hither?
The semiconductor area is down nearly 60 percent since its peak. Frank Husic of Husic Capital Management sees the decline as an opportunity to buy beaten-down companies.

CONTRARIAN

High Velocity
Steve Harmon

Daily Market Rap
Bill Fleckenstein

ThreadTalk
David Zgodzinski

Internet Financial Connection
Mark Johnson

Figure 5-19. Market insight. *(Used with permission of Go2Net, Inc., all rights reserved.)*

Figure 5-20. Active Investment Research. (*Courtesy of StockResearch.com.*)

Active Investment Research

Green Mountain Asset Mgt. Corp.

Useful Web Sites for Investors

For us this is a catch all site. In our opinion, these sites are useful, but we have not yet had the time to break them down into their component parts to save you time so that you can access just the portion that fits your needs. But, if you have the time, there is a lot of information here that is useful to the serious investor.

Financial Institutions

Brokerage Firms

The information at the brokerage firm sites is, not surprisingly, much more useful and often includes nice utilities for calculating IRA data, which can easily be employed for other forms of financial planning.

- PC Financial Network
  Excellent Site–Largest Online Brokerage, Superb Information–A Must Visit/Bookmark
  - Cutter & Co. Brokerage, Inc.
    Midwest Regional Discount Brokerage Firm
  - Fidelity Brokerage Services

- *Main Index (home)*
- *Free Subscription: e-mailed investment newsletter*
- *Buy Recommendations*
- *Investor Education Center*
- *Weekly Economic Update*
- *Investment Philosophy*
- *Historical Results*
- *Data, Quotes and Graphs*

Figure 5-21. Active Investment Research Quick Search. (*Courtesy of StockResearch.com.*)

Active Investment Research

Weekly Economic Update for: January 13, 2001

Part of Our Free Newsletter:
Timely Investment Information

Please Click Here to take our Survey. Thanks.

Financial Market Highlights:

	01/12/01	01/05/01	Change
S & P 500	1,318.56	1,298.34	+1.56%
Dow Jones	10,524.50	10,662.00	-1.29%
NASD Comp	2,626.50	2,407.72	+9.09%
Russell 2000	485.74	463.14	+4.88%

- Main Index (home)
- Free Subscription: e-mailed investment newsletter
- Buy Recommendations
- Investor Education Center
- Treasury Yield Curve
- Investment Philosophy
- Historical Results

Figure 5-22. Weekly economic update. (*Courtesy of StockResearch.com.*)

Figure 5-23. TheStreet.com home page. (*Courtesy of TheStreet.com.*)

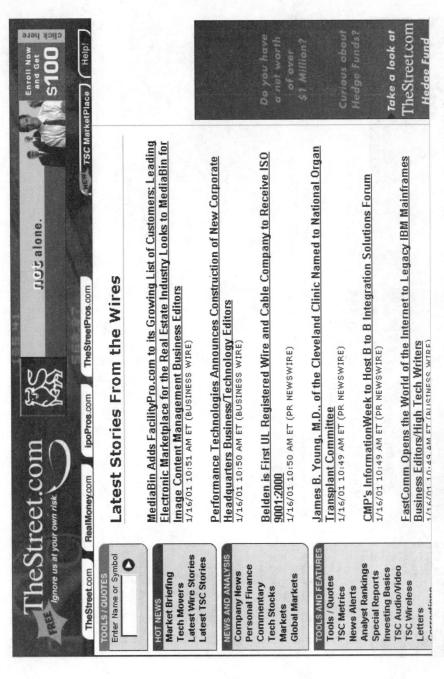

Figure 5-24. Latest stories. (*Courtesy of TheStreet.com.*)

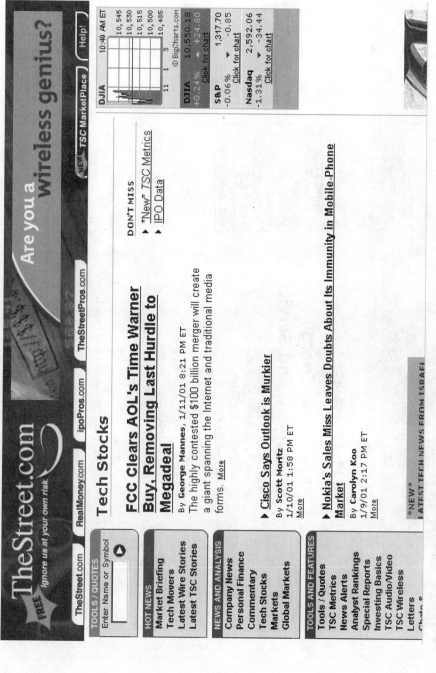

Figure 5-25. Tech report. (*Courtesy of TheStreet.com.*)

109

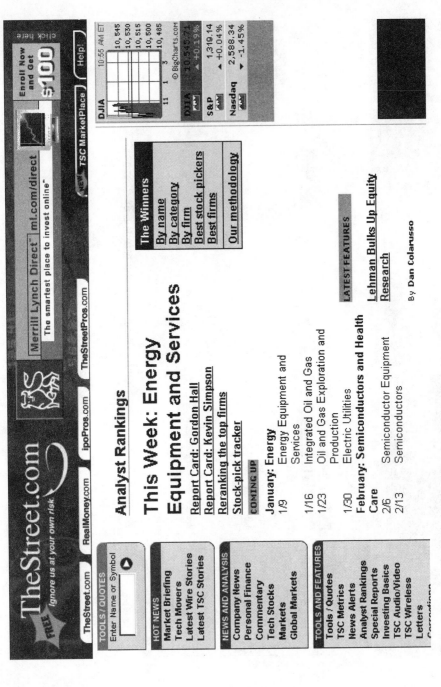

Figure 5-26. Analyst ranking index. (*courtesy of TheStreet.com.*)

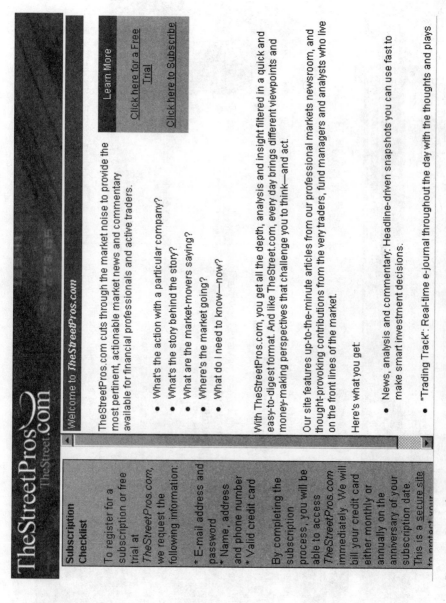

Figure 5-27. TheStreetPros.com subscription site. (*Courtesy of TheStreet.com.*)

Figure 5-28. TradingMarkets.com home page. (*Courtesy of TradingMarkets.com.*)

Figure 5-29. TradingMarkets.com stock commentary. (*Courtesy of TradingMarkets.com.*)

Figure 5-30. TradingMarkets.com news and alerts. (*Courtesy of TradingMarkets.com.*)

114

Figure 5-31. TradingMarkets.com futures education. (*Courtesy of TradingMarkets.com.*)

115

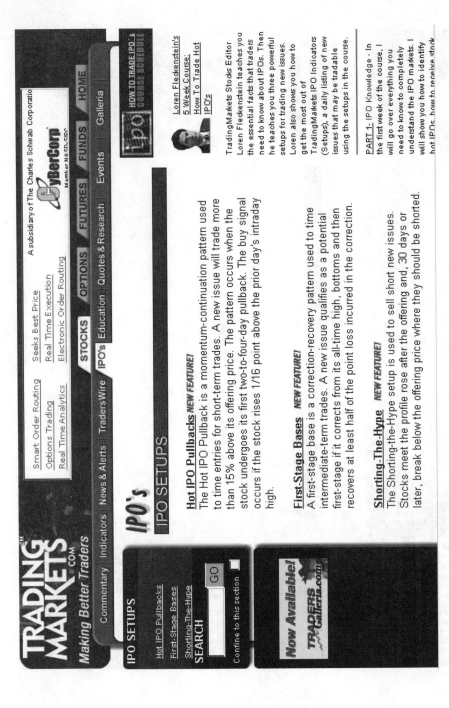

Figure 5-32. TradingMarkets.com stocks: IPOs. (*Courtesy of TradingMarkets.com.*)

6

DIRECT ACCESS TRADING SITES AND FIRMS

Direct access trading can be done at a direct access firm or from the comfort of your own home. Over the course of this chapter we will take you through some of the important questions to ask yourself and to use to evaluation different direct access trading firms and software. Remember, however, that the best test is to actually use a demo of the software or to spend a day at a direct access trading firm.

WHO SHOULD GO TO A DIRECT ACCESS TRADING FIRM?

Individuals who should go to a direct access trading firm are really those considering day trading or trading for a living. If you are only making an occasional trade using direct access trading tools, it really does not pay to spend the time at a direct access trading firm. The real benefits of a direct access trading firm, besides the hardware, software, and connec-

tion speed, is really the environment of other traders. Having other individuals around is one of the best ways to get feedback on your trading
strategies and to find out about new stocks that may be interesting to
trade. In addition, on almost every trading floor there is an air of constant
excitement that flows through as traders yell out comments usually with
some sort of financial news source such as CNBC airing in the background. Any one who has ever been on a trading floor can testify to the
air of excitement that exists. It is a very intense environment, but most
people find it incredibly exhilarating and a lot of fun. Therefore, direct
access trading firms are really ideal for individuals trading for a living or
day traders. This does not mean that you cannot use a direct access trading firm, but the costs probably would not outweigh the benefits you
would receive with such infrequent use.

When you have decided you are going to trade at a direct access
trading firm, there are a bunch of things you need to evaluate. Most
important, you need to find a firm that is best suited to your individual
needs and that has the appropriate technology and environment you are
looking for. Every direct access trading firm is a bit different, and the
individuals in each firm make the environment completely different.
Therefore, over the next couple of pages we will go through some of
the important things to look for when evaluating different direct access
trading firms. There are now even Internet-based trading firms that you
can use solely from the comfort of your own home. As the number of
options for direct access traders continues to increase, we will take a look
at some of the major issues to look at, regardless of whether you phys-
ically trade at a direct access trading firm or trade over the Internet using
a firm's software from the comfort of your own home. Later in this chapter we list the majority of direct access firms at the time of the writing
of this book. Keep in mind, however, that new firms are springing up
all over, and even some of the major online brokerage firms are starting
to offer limited direct access capabilities. The opportunities will only
increase over time. Let's take a look at some of the major things to keep
in mind.

WHY GO TO A DIRECT ACCESS TRADING FIRM?

There are many reasons why to go to a direct access trading firm, but the
number one reason is to make more money. Most individuals find that if
they are around other traders and in the trading environment, they tend

to do better. Then again, there is a small group of other individuals who like to be left to themselves and trade in a very peaceful and tranquil environment. For most direct access traders who are day trading and/or trading for a living, it is very difficult to follow absolutely everything that is happening in the markets. Therefore, by having other individuals around, it is like having extra sets of eyes and ears to find out about new stocks, identify emerging patterns, or simply provide s different viewpoint on where a particular stock is heading. Although some individuals offer better advice than others, it is always interesting to hear what others are saying. But just remember, you always have to develop your trading strategy on your own. Just mimicking someone else who happens to be successful will not make you a great trader or even guarantee you make money, especially in the long term. Individuals who can adapt to the markets by altering their trading strategy are the ones who stand to succeed in the long run. So why go to a direct access trading firm? Direct access trading firms are a great way to enhance your overall knowledge. It basically boils down to your personality traits and what you think of the trading environment. Going to a direct access trading firm can be especially helpful if there is an individual there who will work with you as a mentor. Mentors are the number one best resource for all types of new direct access traders. Make sure to talk to other traders at the trading firms to find out if any of them are open to such a scenario. Each individual reacts differently to these sorts of arrangements, and you usually will not know who would be willing to teach you the ropes until you are there for a little while. All in all, there are many benefits to going to a direct access trading firm if you are going to be devoting your time to day trading and/or trading for a living. Over the next couple of pages we will tell you some of things to look for.

PEOPLE

The first thing to inspect at any direct access trading firm is the people who manage the business and the individuals who actually trade there. You want to make sure the individuals running the office are competent and really provide you with all the tools you need to succeed as a direct access trader. The easiest way to find out if this is the case is obviously by talking to the traders there. Make sure to ask them about the back-end support they receive from the firm and any problems that may have occurred in the past. In addition, ask them about the specific tools they like and dislike about this particular trading firm. And most important, ask how successful the individuals who trade there actually are. This is usually your best indicator and the one that will highlight how good or bad a particular direct access trading firm is.

ENVIRONMENT

The trading environment is another thing to keep a very close eye on when evaluating different direct access trading firms. Are there consistently a good number of individuals there trading, or does the firm appear to be desolate during market hours? Is it a lively environment, or does it appear to be dead? These are all the sorts of things you want to find out well in advance of starting to trade at any direct access trading firm. Because so much of what you are paying for is the environment and the opportunity to be around other traders, you need to make sure that the environment fits your needs.

Please contact these companies for the most up-to-date information and for additional details:

CASTLE ONLINE

URL: *www.castleonline.com*

PHONE: 1-516-868-8812

EMAIL: *paul@castleonline.com*

SERVICES: Free real-time quotes, free proprietary software called MyTrack Basic that includes stock watch, time of sales, portfolio manager, and intraday and other charts.

ACCOUNT MINIMUM: $5000

FEES:

— Level II quote account options ranging from $150 to $300 a month.

— Limit/market trades: $19.95 + $0.01 per share for listed, $19.95 up to 10,000 shares for Nasdaq.

— $1 handling fee from clearing agent for each trade.

— $0.15 per share for any electronic communication network (ECN) other than Island.

SUPPORT: 1-800-661-5133, 1-800-891-1003, or via email.

DAYLIGHT TRADING

URL: *www.daylighttrading.com*
PHONE: 1-800-818-0048
EMAIL: *tradebuddy@hotmail.com, info@daylighttrading.com*

SERVICES: Data Entitlement software, which includes RealTickIII order entry, Nasdaq level II quotes, time of sales, market minders, technical studies, and more. Also provides daily short list.

ACCOUNT MINIMUM: $10,000 plus an average of two trades per day.

FEES:

— $255 per month for Data Entitlement; $30 per month for NYSE data, $35 per month for Amex, and $15 per month for CBOT or CME.

— *Trades:* $14.95 plus ECN fees.

— SOES executions and cancellations, Island, SelectNet free. $0.15 per share for Instinet, BTRD, REDI, and Attain.

SUPPORT: 1-818-242-2119 during market hours, *support@daylighttrading.com.*

DREYFUS BROKERAGE SERVICES, INC.

URL: *www.edreyfus.com*
PHONE: 1-800-421-8395
EMAIL: *support@dreyfus.com*

SERVICES: Dreyfus Remote System offers all major stock market information and includes portfolio analysis on 20-minute delay.

ACCOUNT MINIMUM: $1000; $2000 for options or margin account.

FEES:

— Subscriptions to real-time level II and various Nasdaq screens ranging from $59 to $150 a month.

— *Trades:* $15 per trade up to 10,000 shares. Add $4 per order for private data network.

— No penny stocks or Canadian shares. First three trades free.

SUPPORT: Via toll-free number or email. Also has glossary, sample screens, portfolio demo at Web site.

EQUITY TRADING

URL: *www.equitytrading.com*

PHONE: 1-877-ETTRADE

EMAIL: *info@equitytrading.com*

SERVICES: Three levels of data feed and order entry.

ACCOUNT MINIMUM: $10,000.

FEES:

— Data feed prices vary according to level; from $58.50 to $250 per month.

— Optional new services including Dow Jones news for additional fees.

— *Trades:* $15 per trade up to 1000 shares; $0.15 for every share over 1000.

— ECN charges.

SUPPORT: Toll-free number and email. Demo, in-house seminar, tutorial, glossary.

E*TRADE SECURITIES, INC.

URL: *www.etrade.com*

PHONE: 1-800-ETRADE-1

SERVICES: Free membership to site without opening account includes 100 free real-time quotes daily. Free smart alerts to email or pager. Power E*TRADE account offers real-time quotes, order execution, level II information, and IPO offerings. Touchtone and speech-recognition telephone investing system (1–800-STOCKS-1). Customized portfolio, market watch, and summary statement.

ACCOUNT MINIMUM: $1000; $2000 for margin account.

FEES:

— Free unlimited real-time quotes on login during market hours.

— Limit and stop order trades: $19.95 for up to 5000 shares of listed stocks; then $0.01 per share for entire order. $19.95 for any number of OTC shares. Various investor rebates, discounts when you reach certain number of trades per quarter.

— Market trades: $14.95 for up to 5000 shares of listed stocks; then $ 0.01 per share for entire order. $19.95 for any number of OTC shares.

SUPPORT: 24-hour online customer support. Glossary and demo.

FRANKLIN ROSS, INC.

URL: *www.franklinross.com*

PHONE: 1-877-TRADENOW, 1-877-YESTRADE

EMAIL: *service@franklinross.com*

SERVICES: Level 2 instant order executions.

ACCOUNT MINIMUM: For those making fewer than 150 trades a month: $10,000 to open; $30,000 annual account income; net worth of at least $100,000; one year investment/trading experience. For those making more than 150 trades a month (platinum account): same as above except $50,000 to open.

FEES:

— $308.50 per month for RealTick III trading platform with order entry, level II data, time of sales, charts, Web browser, and NYSE, Nasdaq, and AMEX exchange fees included. Free with platinum account.

— $17.95 per trade up to 10,000 Nasdaq shares or 2000 NYSE/ AMEX shares; $0.01 per share above this. Fees get lower the more trades you make per month; lowest is $13.95 per trade.

— ECN fees: $0.0005 per share to $2.50 per trade depending on ECN.

SUPPORT: Toll-free numbers or via email.

GRO CORPORATION

URL: *www.grotrader.com*

PHONE: 1-800-852-3862

EMAIL: *info@gro.com*

SERVICES: GroTrader, an integrated trading environment for experienced traders, is a real-time, high-end, high-speed trading system. Includes advanced multiple market execution system features, including speed keys, autocancel, close-out, and buy-in functions.

ACCOUNT MINIMUM: $25,000 and 6 months' trading experience.

FEES:

— $19.95 per transaction or $0.02 per share, whichever is greater, for up to 199 trades a month. Prices lower the more trades you make each month; lowest is $14.95 per transaction.

— ECN fees: $0.0025 per share to $2.50 per ticket, depending on ECN.

— Additional exchange fees from $5 to $59.50 (for Nasdaq) per month.

SUPPORT: Toll-free number.

INVESTIN.COM SECURITIES CORP.

URL: *www.investin.com*

PHONE: 1-800-327-1883

EMAIL: *newaccounts@investin.com*

SERVICES: Standard online trading with links to level II quotes. Also offers IPOs online.

ACCOUNT MINIMUM: $1000; $2000 for margin account.

FEES:

— $59 per month for real-time equity quotes; $130 per month for real-time equity, futures, and options quotes. Use of these services increases account minimum to $2000.

— $14.95 per trade plus $0.01 for listed market orders; $19.95 for limit, stop, and Nasdaq orders up to 5000 shares.

SUPPORT: Toll-free number.

INVESTORS STREET

URL: *www.istreet.net*
PHONE: 1-800-327-1883
EMAIL: *traders@investors-street.com*

SERVICES: Real-time NYSE and Nasdaq level II quotes; RealTick for charting and decision support; RealTrade for order entry; live scrolling; alarms with various price limits and alerts; portfolio manager window; and real-time technical studies.

ACCOUNT MINIMUM: None.

FEES:

— Trades: $500 per month or 100 tickets per month for in-house trades; $500 per month or 200 tickets per month for ISDN direct trading; $300 per month for Internet access. $0.02 per share with $18 minimum per trade.

— *ECN fees:* $0.005 per share to $2.50 per trade depending on ECN; added to total commission fee.

SUPPORT: Toll-free number.

LIVESTREET.COM

URL: *www.livestreet.com*

PHONE: 1-516-873-4200

EMAIL: *clientservice@livestreet.com, questions@livestreet.com, techsupportl@livestreet.com*

SERVICES: Real-time trading and portfolio management using RealTick III with live bids/offers, level II data, order execution, position tracking, daily short list, optional Dow Jones news, and customized charts, graphs, and analytics.

ACCOUNT MINIMUM: $10,000; $5000 minimum equity level.

FEES:
— *Data:* $200 per month ($2000 per year prepaid). $60 per month for Nasdaq level II; $50 per month for execution system. $2 to $60 per month for optional exchange fees.
— Call or email for rates; add $0.01 per share for shares over 2000.
— *ECN fees:* range from $0.0005 per share to $0.0025 per trade depending on ECN.

SUPPORT: Via email.

LIVETRADE.COM

URL: *www.livetrade.com*

PHONE: 1-516-873-6640, 1-877-LIVETRADE

EMAIL: *customerservice@livetrade.com,   questions@livetrade.com, techsupportl@livetrade.com*

SERVICES: Live level II market data, choice between RealTick II full-service data feed and order entry, customized ticker, or basic order entry software. Daily short list, free company report and trial subscription to NewsWatch.

ACCOUNT MINIMUM: $25,000 equity to open; $7500 minimum account balance.

FEES:

— *Data:* $324 per month for full data and order entry, $299 per month for preset data and order entry, $112.50 per month for LiveLite order entry only.

— *Trades:* $19.95 for any trade of 100 to 10,000 shares. Destination fees extra.

— *ECN fees:* range from $0.0005 per share to $1 per trade depending on ECN.

SUPPORT: Via email or toll-free phone number.

MARKET WISE TRADING, INC.

URL: *www.marketwisetrading.com*

PHONE: 1-877-MKT-TRADE

EMAIL: *accounts@trademarketwise.com*

SERVICES: Trade Wise Pro for fewer than 5 trades a month; includes real-time quotes, time and sales, technical studies, charting abilities, real-time position and account managers. Trade Wise Elite adds one level II screen; Trade Wise Elite Plus adds ability to use level II information on two equities at same time and has additional market data needed for trading multiple equities simultaneously. Trade Wise Master offers unlimited level II information on many different equities at same time.

ACCOUNT MINIMUM: $5000 for Trade Wise Pro; $25,000 for all others.

FEES:

— *Data:* $160 per month for Pro; $260 per month for Elite; $285 per month for Elite Plus; $325 per month for Master.

— *Trades*: $23 per transaction plus pass-through fees. $0.01 per share on trades of up to 2088 shares on NYSE/AMEX; $0.015 per share for over 2088.

— *ECN fees*: $1 per transaction for ISLD and ARCA.

SUPPORT: Training facilities online.

MAX TRADE LLC

URL: *www.maxtrading.com*

PHONE: 1-248-362-2650

EMAIL: *mailbox@maxtrading.com*

SERVICES: MaxPor, MaxPlus, and MaxPremier all use RealTick III and provide access to Archipelago. Real-time order entry and electronic execution with bids/offers, position minder, tickers, alarms, MultiQuote, and hot keys.

ACCOUNT MINIMUM: $10,000

FEES:

 — *Data:* $100 per month for MaxPro, $175 per month for MaxPlus, $250 per month for MaxPremier. Optional subscription fees for futures and options data.

 — *Trades:* $21.95 per trade for up to 50 trades per month; $20.95 for 51 to 100 trades per month; $19.95 for 100+ trades per month more. Charges do not include ECN destination and exchange fees.

SUPPORT: Toll-free customer service and chat room, customized in-office training.

PACIFIC DAY TRADING, INC.

URL: *www.day-trade.com*

PHONE: 1-408-557-9000

EMAIL: *customerservice@day-trade.com*

SERVICES: Nasdaq level II or NYSE real-time data and Windows software package. Customizable snapshot window and multiple real-time ticker windows, MarketMinder.

ACCOUNT MINIMUM: Check on Web site.

FEES:

 — $350 per month subscription service allows real-time trading on level II or NYSE. Fee waived with average of over 10 fills per day. Remote fees (for when user has own ISP): $175 per month for fixed-page RealTick, $250 per month for full-page RealTick.

— *Limit/market trades:* $02295 per share with $22.95 minimum per fill (which is considered up to 1000 shares at one price level.

— *ECN fees:* Range from $0.0025 per share to $2.50 per fill.

SUPPORT: Basic Training Boot Camp through Electronic Day Trading Services.

POLAR TRADING, INC.

URL: *www.polartrading.com*
PHONE: 1-810-463-0140
EMAIL: *customerservice@polartrading.com*

SERVICES: Polar Trader (full- and fixed-page versions) includes real-time level II and time-of-sales data, customizable charting, instantaneous order entry and trade confirmation, real-time position management, interest list, option quotes, and integrated Web browsers. (Full version also includes Turbo options.) Polar Trader Jr. includes order execution system without level II or time of sales. Mostly for those using other stock analysis applications.

ACCOUNT MINIMUM: $5000.

FEES:

— $230 per month for Polar Trader fixed page for 1 to 19 trades per month, $30 for 20 to 49 trades, free with 50 or more. $300 per month for Polar Trader full page for 1 to 19 trades per month, $100 for 20 to 49 trades, free with 50 or more. $125 per month for Polar Trader Jr., free with 20 trades per month.

— *Trades*: $22.95 per trade for 1 to 19 trades per month; $21.95 per trade for 20 to 49 trades per month; $19.95 per trade for 50 to 99 trades per month; $17.95 per trade for 100 to 199 trades per month; $15.95 per trade for 200 to 399 trades per month; $14.95 for 400+ trades per month. Prices do not include ECN destination charges.

SUPPORT: Via toll-free number, email, and chat room.

RML TRADING

URL: *www.rmltrading.com*

PHONE: 1-888-765-4403

EMAIL: *info@rmltrading.com*

SERVICES: RML Power Trader is a flexible trading platform using a digital market data feed and including Nasdaq level II screens, technical studies and charts, alarms, "smart" quotes, hot keys, BoardView, time of sales, MarketMinder, and more.

ACCOUNT MINIMUM: $10,000.

FEES:

— $250 per month for PowerTrader software plus nonpro exchange fees of $50. Software fees waved after 100 "round-trip" trades per month. Optional news ($75) and ($50) options quotes.

— *Trades:* $14.95 for listed market; $14.95 plus $0.01 per share for listed OTC.

SUPPORT: Live video/audio customer support, in-office trading, full day trader course for $995.

RT DAY TRADING

URL: *www.rttrading.com*

PHONE: 1-800-327-1883

SERVICES: Packages include RT2 (remote trading in real time), RealTick III, and Mercenary Analytics.

ACCOUNT MINIMUM: $10,000.

FEES:

— $300 per month for RT2 Trader with Nasdaq level II and order routing to ECNs; $300 per month for RealTick II with real-time streaming market data and live executions; $79.95 per month for Mercenary Analytics. Free software if trades total 76 to 400 per month; free software and Mercenary if trades exceed 400 per month or 100,000 shares per month.

— *Trades:* $7.95 per trade for up to 100 trades per month; $6.95 per trade for over 100 shares per month. Plus $0.02 per share for up to 25,000 shares per trade; $0.15 per share for 25,001 to 50,000 shares per trade; $0.005 per share for up to 100,001+ shares per trade. $19.95 per trade maximum commission charge.

— Additional ECN/exchange fees.

SUPPORT: Toll-free number, trading seminars.

STOXNOW.COM.

URL: *www.stoxnow.com*
PHONE: 1-877-872-3372
EMAIL: *info@STOXNOW.com*

SERVICES: Online trading system includes instant offer executions combined with level II quotes, charting, tickers, alerts. Short sales routed through staff for approval.

ACCOUNT MINIMUM: $5000.

FEES:

— $340 per month for ProTrader. Rebate of $40 for 10 tickets per month, $300 for 76 tickets per month.

— $16.95 per ticket for up to 100 trades per month; $15.95 for 101 to 200 trades per month.

— Plus $0.008 per share for listed trades.

— *ECN fees:* $0.50 per trade for SOES, $1 per trade for ISLD and SelectNet. Add $0.005 per share for Archipelago.

SUPPORT: Via email. One-on-one training in Scottsdale office.

TERRA NOVA TRADING LLC

URL: *www.terranovatrading.com*
PHONE: 1-800-258-5409
EMAIL: Phone/email directory available on "contact us" page on Web site.

SERVICES: Terra Nova Trader offers dynamically updated, real-time trading and portfolio management adapted from RealTick III, with direct access to Archipelago and customized trading screens.

ACCOUNT MINIMUM: $3000.

FEES:

— $250 per month for Terra Nova Full; $175 per month for Terra Nova Trader Fixed (limited version for one stock; 50 percent rebate with 20 to 49 trades per month; free for 50+ trades per month).

— *Trades:* $22.50 per ticket for 1 to 19 trades per month; $21.95 for 20 to 49 trades per month; $19.95 per ticket for 50 to 99 trades per month; $17.95 per ticket for 100 to 199 trades per month; $16.95 per ticket for 200 to 399 trades per month; $14.95 per ticket for 400+ trades per month.

— Ticket equals 2000 shares. Add $0.015 per share for trades over 2000.

— *ECN fees:* Range from $0.0025 per share to $4 per trade.

SUPPORT: Toll-free technical (1-800-228-4216) and trading support (1-800-452-6294); after-hours trading desk support (1-312-960-1314) and Instinet help (1-312-960-1354).

TRADESCAPE.COM

URL: *www.tradescape.com*

SERVICES: Tradescape PRO answers the needs of active online traders. Built for speed and efficiency from the ground up, it represents a unique union of power and control. Underneath each innovative feature is some of the industry's most sophisticated technology. Together, they create a user-friendly interface for accessing real-time information and order routing tools. Tradescape also offers Lightspeed for professional on-site traders. Lightspeed is the next generation of the FirstLevel™ trading software that is used by thousands of professional on-site traders. This stand-alone trading platform allows remote customers to experience the superior software functionality and performance exclusively available to on-site trading. Lightspeed provides the user with direct connections to ECNs and Nasdaq, "smart" order routing, customization and filter consoles, and thermographs, and allows the user to view the best bids and offers from every ECN, centralized in a single book, and to know the speed of each ECN before trading.

ACCOUNT MINIMUM: $10,000.

FEES:

— Tradescape.com offers a flexible fee schedule that accommodates every online investor. At 1.5 cents per share, a 500-share order will cost just $7.50 in commissions, no matter how many trades it takes to fill the order. Orders of this size often can take multiple orders to fill, and with most online brokerage firms, this can mean multiple commission charges or cancellation fees. The minimum fee per trade is $1.50. For example, if you try to buy 500 shares of Microsoft and you only get filled on 20 shares, your costs for that trade would be $1.50 (plus any ECN or exchange fees). Again, there is no charge for unexecuted or canceled orders. All Tradescape Pro subscribers are required to sign up for level II quotes. If you maintain at least a $25,000 account balance (equity) and execute 50 or more trades per calendar month, level II quotes are completely free. Otherwise, there is a monthly charge of $79.95 ($29.95 plus the $50 exchange fee). All charges, requirements, and refunds refer to the calendar month. Refunds cannot be given for midmonth cancellations.

— *Trades:* For online trading requirements include the following: At least two of the following three minimum requirements: $35,000 annual income, $50,000 liquid net worth, and/or $100,000 in net worth. A $10,000 minimum initial account balance. Existing account holders must maintain a $5000 minimum daily balance. Accounts under this amount will be treated as cash accounts, and margin privileges will be suspended until the minimum account balance of $10,000 is restored. At least 1 year of online trading experience or successfully completing any direct access training program is required (proof of completion of training is necessary). Residence within 1 of the 27 states in which Tradescape.com Securities, through Momentum Securities LLC, is a registered broker-dealer is required. A valid credit card (VISA and

MasterCard only) is required for real-time level II quote fees (free for qualified customers or $79.95 per calendar month). One of the following operating systems is required: Windows NT/2000/ 98/95 (service is not currently available to Mac, Red Hat Linux, or SGI/Solaris Unix users). Browsers: Microsoft Internet Explorer 4.01 or higher or Netscape 4.72.

TREND TRADER

URL: *www.trendtrader.com*

PHONE: 1-888-32-TREND

SERVICES: Order routing and execution; trading through Nasdaq, SOES, and INTO, ISLD, BTRD, REDI, ATTN, and Instinet.

ACCOUNT MINIMUM: $15,000 to open; $10,000 to maintain.

FEES:

— $315 per month for Tors Elite; includes order routing to SOES, ECNs, and Dot; has level II screen and includes NYSE, AMEX, and Opra; allows 80 trades per month.

— $240 per month for Tors Wall Street; includes same but allows 40 trades per month.

— $115 per month for Tors Express; includes same but allows 20 trades per month.

— *Trades:* $25 per ticket for less than 201 trades per month; $22 per ticket for 201 to 400 trades per month; $18 per ticket for 401 to 600 trades per month; $15 per ticket for 600+ trades per month. Prices include additional fees for SOES, SelectNet, and other methods of access.

SUPPORT: Via email and phone; free 1-day demonstration of TORS software at Scottsdale facility.

WEB STREET SECURITIES

URL: *www.webstreet.com*

PHONE: 1-800-WEB-TRADE

EMAIL: *customerservice@webstreetsecurities.com*

SERVICES: Order entry for level I and level II trading; real-time quotes, instant executions (6–10 seconds) on most orders; online pop-up confirmations; monitoring of 10 separate watch lists; unlimited access to baseline company and industry profiles. Premium services offer one-click trading, Nasdaq level II, and streaming quotes.

ACCOUNT MINIMUM: None (except $2000 for margin account).

FEES:

— $29.95 per month for real-time quotes; $50 per month for Nasdaq level II.

— *Trades:* $14.95 for any online limit or market order; $14.95 for less than 1000 shares of any listed Nasdaq stock.

SUPPORT: Full-contact directory online.

1-800-DAYTRADE.COM

URL: *www.1800daytrade.com*
PHONE: 1-800-329-8723
EMAIL: *customerservice@1800daytrade.com*

SERVICES: Wireless trading, daily short list, proprietary software for real-time level I and level II trading.

ACCOUNT MINIMUM: $5000.

FEES:

— $65 per month for futures exchange data; $6 per month for Turbo option quotes; $225 per month for level I quotes, point-and-click order entry (millennium trading gold); $299 per month for level II quotes, real-time charts, balances, point-and-click order entry (millennium trading platinum).

— *Trades:* $14.95 per trade plus $0.02 per share over 2000; $19.95 per ticket for millennium gold/platinum accounts plus $0.01 per share over 2000.

— *ECN Fees:* No charge for ATTN, SOES, ARCA, SNET, ISLD, and TNTO. $0.015 per share for INCA or BTRD. $0.01 per share for AMEX/NYSE.

SUPPORT: Live one-on-one customer service online; live chat.

A.B. WATLEY

URL: *www.abwatley.com*
PHONE: 1-800-229-2853
EMAIL: *newaccount@abwatley.com*

SERVICES: Various levels of software accounts with tiered pricing; touchstone trading for level 1 service; dedicated port service that allows unlimited connection time for $300 per month.

ACCOUNT MINIMUM: $3000 for level 1; $20,000 for levels 2 to 4.

FEES:

— $50 per month for Watley trader; includes free unlimited real-time quotes and $9.95 per trade up to 5000 shares; over 5000, add $0.01 per share for entire order.

— $75 per month for Ultimate Trader Silver; free with over 25 trades per month but does not include charts or level II quotes. $150 per month for Ultimate Trader Gold; free with over 50 trades a month; no level II quotes. $300 per month for Ultimate Trader Platinum; includes RealTick streaming quotes, Nasdaq level II screens, charts.

— *Trades:* $23.95 per trade for 1 to 9 trades per month; $22.95 per trade for 10 to 24 trades per month; $20.95 per trade for 25 to 49 trades per month; $19.95 for 50 to 99 trades per month; $18.95 per trade for 100 to 199 trades per month; deep discounts for above 199 trades per month. Add $0.01 per share for more than 2000 listed shares and more than 10,000 Nasdaq shares.

— *ECN Fees:* Extra $0.015 per share for INCA, REDI, TNTO, and ATTN; extra $0.005 per share for BTRD; $1.25 per ticket for Selectnet.

SUPPORT: Toll-free, priority-client-only phone number.

ALL-TECH INVESTMENT GROUP, INC.

URL: *www.attain.com*

PHONE: 1-888-328-8246

EMAIL: *trade@attain.com*

SERVICES: Nasdaq level II real-time market data; market monitoring by customizable analytical programs.

ACCOUNT MINIMUM: $25,000 for active day trading; $15,000 for casual trading; $10,000 for retail accounts.

FEES:

— $250 per month software commission; waived at 200 transactions per month.

— *Trades:* $25 per transaction for Nasdaq; same for listed except add $0.005 per share up to 2000 shares and $0.015 for 2001 shares and above.

— *ECN fees:* Free for ATTN; $1 per ticket for SelectNet and ISLD; extra $0.015 per share for BTRD, REDI, BRUT, and INCA; $0.005 per share for TNTO; REDI and BRUT not available.

SUPPORT: 1-877-925-5832.

ANDOVER TRADING

URL: *www.andovertrading.com*

PHONE: 1-800-788-2717 and 1-888-398-2638

EMAIL: *trade@attain.com*

SERVICES: In-office Prentium processors with Pro 400 and 21-inch monitors; real-time quote/order system.

ACCOUNT MINIMUM: $50,000 minimum recommended to begin trading.

FEES:

— *Trades:* $8 per online trade, $18 per broker-assisted trade; ECN charges additional.

— *In-house commissions:* OTC: $20 for 10 to 20 shares, $18 for 21 to 30 shares, $17 for 31 to 40 shares, $16 for 41 to 60 shares, $15 for 61 to 80 shares, $14 for 81+ shares. NYSE: $10 plus $0.125 per share for 1 to 5 million shares, $10 plus $0.01 per share for above 5 million shares.

SUPPORT: Toll-free numbers to live representatives.

BROADWAY TRADING LLC

URL: *www.broadwaytrading.com*
PHONE: 212-328-3555
EMAIL: *info@daytrading.com*

SERVICES: Offices in New York City, Long Island, and Boca Raton, FL. Proprietary trading system (Watcher) offers Nasdaq level II quotes and execution, position monitoring, and access to Island ECN.

ACCOUNT MINIMUM: $75,000 (cash or marginable securities).

FEES:
— *Trades:* from $0.02 to $0.04 per share per trade.

SUPPORT: 1-212-328-3555; *support@broadwaytraining.com;* hands-on training to learn to use Watcher tool.

CYBER BROKER, INC.

URL: *www.cybercorp.com*
PHONE: 1-512-322-5444

SERVICES: Three account styles, trading rooms, charting, and technical analysis; trading through CyBerXchange, a proprietary intelligent central order routing and execution system.

ACCOUNT MINIMUM: $25,000 for active day trading; $15,000 for casual trading; $10,000 for retail accounts.

FEES:

— *CyBerTrader/CyberT account:* $250 per month for up to 99 tickets; free with 100 or more tickets per month. $15,000 trading capital to open, maintain daily equity balance of $7500, minimum annual income of $50,000, and net worth of $100,000 exclusive of home. Includes real-time level II data.

— *CyBerX account:* $49 per month for up to 50 tickets per month; free with 51 or more tickets per month. $10,000 trading capital to open, maintain daily equity balance of $5000, minimum annual income of $35,000, net worth of $65,000 exclusive of home. Includes real-time level I data.

— *Trades:* $19.95 per ticket for up to 199 tickets per month; $18.95 per ticket for 200 to 299 tickets per month; $17.95 per ticket for 300 to 399 tickets per month; $16.95 per ticket for 400 to 499 tickets per month; $15.95 per ticket for 500 to 599 tickets per month; $14.95 per ticket for 600 or more tickets per month.

— *ECN fees:* Free for SOES and Island Direct; add $1 per trade for SelectNet Direct or Attain Direct; $250 per trade for SelectNet Broadcast; $0.0025 per share for ISLD and REDI; $0.015 per share for BRUT, INCA; $0.005 per share for ATTN, BTRD, TNTO, and NYSE.

SUPPORT: 1-512-320-8930 for technical assistance; 1-512-320-0833 for trading assistance; 1-512-320-5444 for training assistance.

DELTA TRADER

URL: *www.deltatrader.com*

PHONE: 1-888-781-0283

EMAIL: *customerservice@1800daytrade.com*

SERVICES: Before- and after-hours trading via Instinet; Delta Trader PRO is software-based execution system with real-time snap quotes and intraday portfolio updates.

ACCOUNT MINIMUM: $5000 for Delta Trader PRO; $1000 for Delta Trader, which is a browser-based online trading system.

FEES:

— Trades: $7.75 per trade for OTC.

— *Listed:* $0.02 per share for market orders, $0.03 per share for limit orders. $15 per trade minimum.

SUPPORT: Toll-free number.

DLJ DIRECT

URL: *www.DLJdirect.com*

PHONE: 1-877-355-5557

EMAIL: *service@dljdirect.com*

SERVICES: After-hours trading for Select Clients; proprietary MarketSpeed software includes real-time order execution, customizable investing tools, and other features.

ACCOUNT MINIMUM: None. Select Clients must maintain $1 million in assets in combined DLJ Direct accounts.

FEES:

— *Trades:* $20 per trade up to 1000 shares plus $0.02 per share above this amount. Various fees for penny stocks, mutual funds, options, and margin.

— *In-house commissions:* OTC: $20 for 10 to 20 shares, $18 for 21 to 30 shares, $17 for 31 to 40 shares, $16 for 41 to 60 shares, $15 for 61 to 80 shares, $14 for 81+ shares. NYSE: $10 plus $0.125 per share for 1 to 5 million shares; $10 plus $0.01 per share for above 5 million shares.

SUPPORT: Email and 24-hour customer support at 1-800-825-5723.

EDGETRADE SECURITIES LLC

URL: *www.edgetrade.*

PHONE: 1-888-440-3343

EMAIL: *info@edgetrade.com*

SERVICES: Real-time inside quotes for Nasdaq level II and NYSE; access to execution system, live confirmation, technical data, etc.

ACCOUNT MINIMUM: $25,000.

FEES:

— $280 per month for TradeCast plus exchange fees of $58.50 per month. Both free with over 150,000 shares traded per month.

— *Trades:* $0.055 per share for up to 3999 shares; $0.035 per share for 4000 to 4999 shares; $0.025 per share for 10,000 to 19,999 shares; $0.02 per share for over 20,000 shares per day. Further price breaks for high-volume traders.

— *ECN fees:* $0.015 per share for BRUT, INCA; $0.01 per share for NYSE/AMEX; $0.005 per share for ATTN, BTRD, TNTO, REDI.

SUPPORT: Live online help during market hours, toll-free number, email.

INSIDER TRADING

URL: *www.insder-trading.net*
PHONE: 1-516-951-1638
EMAIL: *clients@mbtrading.com*

SERVICES: Real-time quotes, level II market data, direct execution ability on Nasdaq and NYSE/AMEX, charts, news, etc.

ACCOUNT MINIMUM: $5000, of which $1000 must be in cash.

FEES:

— *Trades:* Rates begin at $21.95; $10 extra for call-in trades.

— *ECN fees:* $2.75 per trade for ARCA; $0.015 per share for ATTN and Bloomberg; $0.0075 per share for Instinet; $0.0025 per share for Island; $0.01 per share for listed; $0.015 per share for REDI; $0.50 per trade for 1000 shares or less on Nasdaq.

SUPPORT: Through AOL's Instant Messenger from 9 A.M. to 7 P.M. EST.

MB TRADING, INC.

URL: *www.mbtrading.com*

PHONE: 1-888-790-4800 or 1-310-414-9299

EMAIL: *customersvcs@insder-trading.net*

SERVICES: Three levels data configuration with real-time trading and portfolio management using RealTick III and level II data.

ACCOUNT MINIMUM: $2000.

FEES:

— Fees vary from $300 per month to no charge depending on which level of data (MB Trader, MB Custom, or MB Lite) you choose and how frequently you trade. (Fees waived after either 20 or 50 trades per month.)

— *Trades:* $22.95 per trade for 1 to 19 trades per month; $21.95 per trade for 20 to 49 trades per month; $19.95 per trade for 40 to 99 trades per month; $17.95 per trade for 100 to 199 trades per month; $16.95 per trade for 200 to 399 trades per month; $14.95 per trade for 400 or more trades per month. Add $0.01 per share for listed issues.

— *ECN per exchange fees:* $65 futures exchange fee (waived after 50 trades per month); no charge for all other exchange fees. All ECN fees included except $0.015 per share for Instinet trades.

SUPPORT: 24-hour-day phone support.

SUNLOGIC SECURITIES, INC.

URL: *www.sunlogic.com*

PHONE: 1-800-556-4600

SERVICES: After-hours trading, limited to 30 minutes before Nasdaq opens and 45 minutes after NYSE closes. Order entry and trade status on same screen, electronic confirmation, free real-time quotes.

ACCOUNT MINIMUM: $2000.

FEES:

- *Limit trades:* $0.01 per share for Nasdaq, $0.02 for listed stock,; $32 minimum trade.
- *Market trades:* $15.99 for Nasdaq plus $0.02 per share for listed stock.
- Various fees for after-hours and broker-assisted trades and options.

SUPPORT: Toll-free number, Sunlogic research, Bloomberg market report.

SUMMARY

The number of new direct access trading sites and firms continues to increase rapidly. Each one is different in the type of software it uses, the technology, and the hardware. In addition, each direct access trading firm has its own unique feel to its environment based on the traders it has. The most important thing to remember is that although there are so many new firms offering direct access trading tools, many eventually will not make it. There is a reason that people invest their money with Fidelity, Goldman Sachs, Morgan Stanley, and other big-name brokerage firms. Although it is impossible for any direct access trading firm to have built such a name in the short period of time direct access trading has been possible, there are still a couple that stand above the rest. This does not mean that you cannot go out and experiment with a lesser-known firm, but do your homework very carefully. Most important, get the feedback of other traders working there or using the firm's software. Also, how well are the traders doing? Although this may sound extremely materialistic, the best traders who are making the most money usually stick together.

The first decision to make is whether you plan on trading from home or going to a direct access trading firm. It is important to note that as of right now, most direct access trading firms are located in major cities. Therefore, if you do not live near a major city, you may have no option but to trade from home. Fear not, the Internet will enable you to create a "trading-like" environment by linking up with other traders across the nation. For individuals who are considering day trading on any level, it is recommended that you go to an actual firm. This is not a must, and many individuals successfully day trade from their own living rooms, but many more individuals say that having other traders around them makes them a better trader. By having other traders around, they feel the pulse of the market, learn about other stocks, and have someone to discuss strategies and charts with on a consistent basis. For individuals who are going to be using direct access trading tools at home, the most important thing to do is to get set up with the right hardware and software from the beginning. There are now many firms that offer Web-based direct access trading software. Although each will tout its own as the "latest and greatest," it is imperative that you do your own homework and get the opinions of other traders. And any trader who does not tell you any negatives about any given software product is lying. Every trader always wishes his or her software did something different in addition to what it already does. Most firms also will let you have a trial period with their tools or software. Never sign up for anything that locks you into an extended agreement unless you have an adequate amount of time to try out the products and services first. As you navigate through the choices of direct access trading sites and firms, remember to look for one that best suits your specific needs. Even within the world of direct access trading, there are so many different types of traders, and each site or firm is usually focused on a particular type.

Education

Trading education has become much more popular as the number of online traders has increased. In fact, many online brokerage firms are now either requiring that traders have taken a course or are strongly suggesting that they do so. Tradescape seems to have taken the lead, requiring that traders submit written proof of graduation from a trading course. Beyond coursework, there has been a surge of conferences, educational software, and social clubs. This section details these different educational opportunities.

Trading schools come in a number of forms, ranging from in-person seminars to CD-ROMs. Trading education is offered either from brokerage firms or from companies that only do training; there are costs and benefits to each. Online brokerage firms usually only offer training on their own software, meaning that you should research the firm before you sign up for the course. If you do not think that you will want to trade with that firm, then it may be best to look for a course elsewhere. However, these firms do have the advantage of being the most knowledgeable about their own software, and learning how to use software is critical to success. If you like the firm, it may be best to learn from it directly. Below are some detailed descriptions of the types of learning experiences offered. There are, of course, many different companies other than the ones listed here. It is important to review your options before choosing any one of them.

All-Tech Training Group, Inc., www.traintotrade.com.

All-Tech Training Group offers an extensive course schedule. To ease geographic constraints, All-Tech has developed an Internet-based training course that meets in a virtual classroom in real time. Led by a moderator, the class meets online for 3 hours in the evening from Monday to Friday. Cost is $495, and only basic computer experience is usually required. The curriculum familiarizes new traders with the latest direct access electronic trading software. All-Tech also offers ATTAIN Basics, a weekend course that focuses on navigating the Real Tick and ATTAIN systems, executing trades, routing systems, routing and shorting rules for the Nasdaq and NYSE, and margin rules for day trading. This course costs $495, and the course is given in Seattle, WA, and Montvale, NJ.

All-Tech also has developed training courses for more experienced traders in its Strategy Mechanics Analysis Rules and Theory Traders Education (SMART) Program. SMART Bootcamp is an intense, 7-day course that covers, among many topics, risks, interpreting Nasdaq level I and II data, and identifying momentum. The course meets Saturday and Sunday, 9 A.M. to 5 P.M., and Monday to Friday, 9:30 A.M. to 4:30 P.M., and costs $3000. Students must have the approval of an All-Tech advisor. A second program, the SMART Four-Phase Program is a more comprehensive course for traders with some experience. Traders learn from instructors and take exams; an exam is needed to graduate from the second and third phrases. Students are critiqued by instructors. The class costs $5000 and meets Monday to Friday, 9:00 A.M. to 4:30 P.M.; students are generally allowed to move through the four phases at their own pace. All-Tech also offers continuing education and personalized training, both free to graduates of other All-Tech programs.

Market Wise Trading School, www.getmarketwise.com.

Beyond its services as an online brokerage firm, Market Wise also operates the Market Wise Stock Trading School. The school offers a number of educational classes. David Nassar, author of *How to Get Started in Electronic Day Trading*, has created a home study course of trading strategies with McGraw-Hill. The course features over 10 hours of audio, a CD-ROM, and a 275-page manual, all focused on the nuts and bolts of trading strategy. For those just starting out, Market Wise also offers a Four-Day Advanced Electronic Strategy course for $2995, also led by Nassar. The courses take place across the country and offer a complete explanation of trading, beginning with the differences between online investors and traders and ending with trading strategies. The course also instructs on how to use trading software. For those who have already begun trading, there is also an Advanced Options course.

Pristine Day Trader, www.pristine.com.

Pristine offers a wide variety of trader education. Developed and led by Pristine gurus Oliver Velez and Greg Capra, Pristine offers 1-day boot camps, 3-day seminars, and 2-week seminars. One and three-day seminars serve to educate traders about tactics and strategies and are geared toward both short- and long-term traders. The seminars also spend time teaching students how to interpret charts and how to use Pristine's method of swing trading, i.e., of holding stocks for 2 to 5 days. Seminars are 9 hours each day. The 2-week seminar is held in Pristine's Seattle office, costs $3500, and is limited to eight students. The course is an intense introduction, designed to help beginners begin trading as soon as they have finished the course. Classes are 5 hours each day. Pristine also has opened up a training center in its home office in White Plains, NY, where prospective and active traders can learn from the pros in 6-month mentorship programs.

Sceptre Trading, www.sceptretrading.com.

Sceptre Trading prides itself on not being an online brokerage firm. It offers both a home and a classroom course. The classroom course meets at the home office in Dallas, TX, where the company trade its own stocks. The program meets for a week, with 3 hours of class each day. The rest of the time is spent on the trading floor, learning from the traders themselves. The class covers the basics of direct access trading. Cost is $3000. The home course package is taught by videocassette and teaches the same fundamentals as the classroom course, without the live experience on the floor. The six VHS tapes contain over 10 hours of instruction; cost is $495.

Direct Access Trading Conferences

International Online Trading Expo, www.onlinetradingexpo.com.

The International Online Trading Expo is an annual conference that brings together the best in the industry. The conference lasts from Friday to Sunday, and in 2000, the conference in New York City attracted some 5200 traders from all 50 states and 39 countries. The conference features several major speeches by industry leaders; the next conference, in Ontario, CA, will showcase Philip Berber, founder and CEO of CyBer-Corp.com and one of the most renowned people in the business. The conference is largely educational; attendees may go to 6 of the 36 tutorials offered, on subjects ranging from execution systems to stock picking to technical analysis. A handbook is also given out with the notes from all the tutorials. These tutorials are always taught by professional traders or authors. In addition, the conference has a large showroom where new products and services are demonstrated. On Friday during market hours, many vendors show their products working during actual trading. The cost for entrance into the conference is $400 and is $469 with a reception. The showroom may be entered without registering for the conference, for a cost of $50.

Technical Analysis Group (TAG), www.ino.com/tag/.

TAG is the longest running conference on trading stocks, futures, and options, having begun in 1978. This 4-day annual conference brings over 30 market experts into Dallas, TX, and promises personal instruction from some of the industry's best. The conference also features several preconference workshops on a variety of topics and four special workshops limited to several traders. Cost is $890 for the full and preconferences; $1140 for the special workshop, full and preconferences; $295 for the preconference only; $695 for the full conference only; and $445 for the special workshop. And of course, a complete showroom of new products is open to everyone.

FIA Expo, www.fiafii.org.

FIA is the association representative of most organizations involved in the futures market, with over 200 corporate members. Every November in Chicago, FIA holds its annual conference, featuring conferences and speeches on the futures market and a large showroom. It is the largest futures industry event. Many new products make their first appearance here. Much of the conference discusses brokerage issues and strategies. Entrance into the conference is $450.

Computer Software

While many companies have entered the market of online and in-person classes, few have ventured into educational trading software. Due to the many changes made to the industry recently, few companies have been willing to create software that may soon be outdated. Good software allows prospective traders to learn on their own schedule, an important bonus for people who cannot take 2 weeks to go to a seminar. It is also much cheaper than actual classes. There are several companies who have created software that is becoming more widely used; they are described below. Educational software can be very helpful, but you should always conduct a little bit of background research before purchasing it. If possible, find reviews of the software to see what others think about it. Also, make sure that your computer meets the hardware requirements for the software to run properly. Many software companies allow trial sessions for free. This is always a good idea and will allow you test it before actually making the purchase.

Online Trading Academy, www.tradingacademy.com.

In addition to other educational services, the Online Trading Academy has developed educational software. The 8-hour multimedia interactive CD, "Fundamentals of Trading Course," has been called ". . . the best explanation of online trading" by *Stocks and Commodities Magazine.* Topics range from trading terminology and psychology to charting and trading styles. Two different versions have been created for specific direct access brokers, CyBerCorp and Tradescape.

SpecTrader+ by Cavlogix Corporation.

SpecTrader+ offers the opportunity to buy and sell stocks, bonds, currencies, and penny stock securities in different randomly generated market scenarios, all without losing a dime. The simulation software allows players to test their trading and investing skills and can work for almost any level of experience. SpecTrader+ allows players to set the scenario for beginner, intermediate, or expert. The game comes with a 40-page manual and a 3-inch floppy disk. Cost is $39.95 to have a physical copy sent by mail; $19.95 for an electronic version sent via email.

Social Groups

As online trading has increased in the past few years, new social groups have emerged that try to unite traders on a local and national level. The clubs have frequent weekend meetings (not during trading hours, of course), often led by guest speakers. They also allow traders to interact with each other and form valuable professional contacts. The membership fees to these clubs are very reasonable, and the benefits are very good. Speaking with others can be the most the most educational opportunity available, and it is certainly worth exploring.

Day Traders USA, www.worldwidetraders.com.

Day Traders USA is the premier social organization that brings traders together for social gatherings, educational talks, and networking. There are currently chapters in over 20 states; once an area has 35 interested traders, Day Traders USA will assist in organizing a chapter. Chapters usually have weekly meetings on the weekends that feature speakers. A schedule from Day Traders of Orange County listed Jeff McKee as the featured speaker on the topic of "Seven Trading Rules." Besides speakers, most events set aside an hour for traders to mingle and talk with each other. Annual membership is around $100, although Day Traders USA frequently lowers it to attract newcomers. Membership allows a trader to attend meetings and also to access a wide variety of resources on the Day Traders USA Web page, including recorded strategy presentations, "Ninja Report" with condensed financial news, and study tutorials.

American Association of Individual Investors, www.aaii.org.

A nonprofit organization, the American Association of Individual Investors (AAII) focuses on providing education in stock investing, mutual funds, and portfolio management. Currently, there are over 60 chapters in the United States. The AAII sends out a monthly newsletter, and individual chapters hold weekly or bimonthly meetings, often featuring speakers. A listing from the Charlotte, NC, chapter noted a speech by John Simms, chief investment office at Stearns Financial Services Group, on the topic of "Mid-Year 2000 Investment Outlook: Short-Run Volatility versus Long-Run Promise." The AAII also offers weekend seminars and retreats, open to members of all chapters. There are national events on almost three weekends of every month. Membership is inexpensive: $49 to receive all AAII correspondence by mail and $39 to receive it electronically. Both memberships allow investors to attend meetings and conferences and give them access to secured areas on the AAII Web site. While the group includes all types of investors, there is a substantial population of direct access traders.

QUESTIONS TO ASK YOURSELF

1   What type of direct access trader do you plan on being?
2   Do you plan on day trading?
3   Do you plan on trading from home or trading at a direct access trading firm?
4   If you are planning on trading from home, what will you need to get to establish your trading environment?
5   If you are planning on trading from home, what can you do to re-create the trading environment?
6   What are the important specs you are looking for in direct access trading software?
7   Do you know any individuals who are currently at a direct access trading firm or using direct access trading software?
8   How many individuals trade there?

QUESTIONS FOR A DIRECT ACCESS TRADING FIRM

1   Is there ever a case when there is not the hardware available to trade on any given day?
2   What are the specifications of the computer hardware that you use?
3   What trading software do you use?
4   What sort of Internet connection do you have?
5   What hours are the offices open?
6   How do the fees work, and what are the other additional costs?
7   Are there traders here who enjoy being mentors for new direct access traders?

7

QUESTIONS AND ANSWERS

Q: Why have most people not heard about direct access trading and ECNs?

A: Most people may not have heard of these terms directly, but they have probably heard of other terms that relate to them. Day trading is one example. Day traders have been the early adopters in using these tools to give themselves an edge in the markets and make intraday trades. What is most fascinating, though, is that the technology is now readily available to anyone; it is just that day traders got to it first. Direct access trading tools allow individuals to bypass the "middleman," have access to a whole new level of information, and ultimately get the best price for their trade. Over the next couple of years, more and more people will start knowing about direct access trading. Even some of the large online brokerage firms are starting to offer after-hours trading, which is essentially this technology. Direct access trading is the way of the future, and it is gaining steam really fast.

Q: Is direct access trading the same thing as day trading?

A: Definitely not. Direct access traders use the same tools as day traders but in many cases are doing something very different. Although day trading is what brought the tools and technology behind direct access trading into the limelight, they can be used for so many different things. At its most basic level, direct access trading tools allow individuals to eliminate the "middleman" and trade directly with another individual. This creates a lower transaction cost and allows someone to get in on a price at his or her own terms. There is no such thing as a market order. If you see a price that you want, you "hit" it, and you own it or you sell it. As time goes on, so many people will be using direct access trading tools that it will just become another normal part of trading or investing—just like online investing evolved. This is just the next logical step. Some day the technology behind direct access trading tools will allow people to exchange all types of securities, not just stocks, on a one-to-one worldwide basis. It will be amazing.

Q: Who is direct access trading for?

A: Direct access trading makes the most sense for individuals who are trading pretty frequently. They do not have to be a day trader, but making a trade once a quarter really does not quality. It also makes a lot of sense if you like to get in on initial public offerings (IPOs) or are trading large blocks of stocks. So really anybody who is making somewhat frequent trades is suited for direct access trading. You just have to have the patience to take the proper time to learn the ropes from the beginning instead of just jumping in. All the stories you hear about day traders who lost all their money occur because they just jumped in with no training and no discipline. It takes time to learn how to use direct access trading tools, and it is not as easy as you might think. On the other hand, if it were that easy, everybody would be using it, and you would not have that edge once you master the basics yourself.

Q: What was the hardest part for you in terms of mastering the tools of direct access trading?

A: When I started, I was completely overwhelmed with the amount of information I all of a sudden had available to me. However, quickly I learned how to sort through all of it and get to what I need. I really just spent a lot of time in the beginning learning the basics like level II quotes and who the market makers were. Also, I spent a lot of time mastering my keystrokes on the keyboard. Speed is the name of the game in direct access trading; this is what your entire advantage is based on whether you are a long-term direct access trader or a day trader. However, besides this, it really just took time to iron out my trading strategy. The tools are not that difficult to learn once you know where to look and how to use them. Just like anything else, it takes a bit of time to get used to, but now I could never trade without them. In fact, I cannot believe that I ever did now.

Q: What is the difference behind the technology involved with online investing and direct access trading?

A: The main difference is that you are not using a third party to place the trade. You are essentially trading with another individual somewhere else in the world directly. Therefore, there is no waiting to find out if your order was ever executed or putting in a "market order." You see a price, and you take it; this is if you want it. Most people are pretty naive to the fact that when they see a stock quote, it is basically a summary of all the other prices out there. In addition, most of them do not even see it real time, which is another considerate disadvantage they have. The technology behind them is fairly similar, but you are really just alleviating the "middleman."

Q: What advantages does direct connectivity provide?

A: Being a direct access trader means that you have access to the same information as Wall Street professionals. People at home placing their trade through an online broker really do not realize what a disadvantage they are at. You are essentially paying more for a slower service. Now granted, direct access trading is probably not for an 83-year-old grandmother, but if you are comfortable with learning new skills and the speed of direct access trading, you can really put yourself at an advantage in the markets. This does not guarantee that you will make money, but you will at least have tools as good as anyone else out there.

Q: How has the technology changed for direct access trading over the last couple of years?

A: The technology behind direct access trading has evolved due to various measures enforced by the Securities and Exchange Commission (SEC) as of the last couple of years to break down the elite "clubs" on Wall Street who had the inside scoop for so long. In addition, the advent of the Internet and faster-speed connections to it means that individuals worldwide can now have a ringside seat to Wall Street. The tools used by Wall Street professionals in the past were extremely expensive and were prohibitive even to new firms entering the marketplace. Fortunately, technology has changed all of this, and now you can trade using direct access from anywhere with an Internet connection.

Q: How is it being used now by others besides day traders?

A: Day traders were some of the first individuals to use direct access trading. They got a lot of attention, although not all positive, because of the fact that many of them were making a lot of money and others were losing a lot of money. The technology behind direct access trading is the same technology that day traders use. These other individuals are basically just using it more conservatively. There are a lot of misconceptions about day traders, but you can really use the technology to do so many different things, and some day, whether we know it or not, we all will.

Q: What are the specs of hardware that you should be using to access the markets directly?

A: Once again, it really depends. You should really have a fairly new computer that has enough memory so that you are not waiting for information to be pulled up. However, this does not mean you should run out and buy a new computer. Most computers, if you bought them in the last year or two, will do just fine. In addition, you want to make sure that you have a monitor that is big enough for you to comfortably display a lot of information. Most direct access trading screens allow individuals to have a number of windows minimized in different corners of the screen so that they can make out plenty of information. Whether you have a laptop or a normal desktop computer, make sure you have at least a 14-inch screen.

Q: What are the different types of software available to access the markets directly?

A: Well, you really do not need software per se to access the markets directly any more. You can now do it directly over the Internet with, say, Tradescape 1.0. Therefore, you do not need to do anything special to your computer, and you can access the markets from anywhere with a computer and an Internet connection. However, obviously, there are places that still use software for trading, news retrieval, and other things. The key once again is to really customize what is available and talk to other traders and get their feedback. Some systems are easier to use than others, whereas others just provide way too much information. Most companies will let you demo their software, but more important, find other unbiased traders who use it and get their opinions.

Q: How important is it to have a fast Internet connection?

A: Some traders are comfortable using a standard 28.8-K or 58.6-K connection; however, it really is an advantage to have access to DSL, a T-1, or some other faster sort of connection. The advantage you have as a direct access trader is real-time information and the ability to execute your trades immediately, so why forfeit a component of your speed advantage? Many people, however, especially long-term direct access traders, can still get by without it. For them especially, it is not absolutely necessary. But if you are a day trader for a living, you probably should get it. You probably can get something like DSL for around $60 a month at home, or any direct access trading firm *definitely* should have it already. If a direct access trading firm does not, this is a great example of a red flag. Just turn around immediately.

Q: What are the different types of analytical tools that are especially helpful for traders?

A: It really depends on whether you are trading for the long or short term. If you are trading for the short term, it is extremely important because you probably will rely on technical analysis for almost all your trading decisions. Therefore, being able to understand different patterns that emerge in the stock and look for signs of how the stock has reacted in the past to certain events and price levels are extremely important. If you are a long-term direct access trader, you are probably using more fundamental analysis, and analytical tools therefore will not be that important to you. Although it is always good to having a working knowledge of certain analytical tools, do not get too bogged down in them if you are a long-term direct access trader. If you are planning on being a day trader, however, you have to learn the basics, like head and shoulder movements and being able to detect momentum. But do not think you have to have a degree in business to get into this. Personally, I was an English major in college and was just fascinated by the markets. It took me some time to learn the basics, but it was not rocket science. It was really more important that I did have a love of and fascination for the markets in general.

Q: How should you decide whether or not to go to a direct access trading firm?

A: It really depends. Some traders I know could never trade without having other people around them. Others really like to be by themselves when they trade. I would say that if you plan on making this your profession, it probably makes the most sense to go to a direct access trading firm. This is mostly because it forces you to get up every morning and out of your house and into a routine. The one thing I hear guys saying is that when they trade from home, they get sidetracked much more easily. If you are going to make direct access trading your profession, then you need to treat it like a very serious full-time job. Although the hours are not so bad, they are as intense as if you were performing surgery the entire time. Your brain must be continuously on and very focused. If you are planning on using the tools for your normal trading on a part-time basis, then I would say there is probably not too much of a need to go into a direct access trading firm. You can get set up pretty well at home just by having the right computer, software, and a fast Internet connection.

Q: How important is speed for direct access traders?

A: Speed is the number one advantage of direct access traders. It is still amazing to me that individuals are trading using delayed quotes at home. Even if they are just putting in a market order for 100 shares of Microsoft, they could save $50 or even $100 dollars if they had more real-time information. It is not just being able to see what the actual "real" price of the stock is, it is being able to have access to a wealth of other real-time information such as breaking news or analyst recommendations. Basically, when I place an order, I do not have to wait for a third party to confirm or tell me that a trade was placed. More important, for a market order, I do not have to give them an upper or lower limit in terms of what I am willing to pay. I see the price I want, and I have the tools to immediately buy or sell the stock. No one at home using a broker or a normal online investing firm can do this. This speed gives me an incredible edge in the markets. This is part of the reason why it is also really important to have a fast connection to the Internet. Why give yourself the advantage of having direct access tools and then slow yourself down by using a 28.8-K modem? Regardless of what type of trader you are, take advantage of speed in every instance you can.

Q: What should people be looking for when evaluating the different direct access options?

A: Well, basically, it really depends on what you are looking to do. If you want to be a day trader, you probably should go to a firm that has the best tools possible and a great group of people for you to be around. If you are looking to be a long-term direct access trader, it usually makes more sense to just trade from the comfort of your own home. It is always good to be around other individuals, but it really depends on how much you are going to be putting into it. You really have to decide what you are going to put into it.

Q: What are some of the things you need to be careful of?

A: The key is not to get carried away with direct access trading tools once you get the hang of it. Do not start day trading just because you feel you understand how to use the tools now. Direct access trading tools are very powerful, and you should really make sure to use them only for trades you are qualified to do. The other thing is to just really make sure you spend some time on a simulator before you go live.

Q: Tell me a little about the level II screen and what is shows traders?

A: A level II screen shows level II quotes, which essentially are the inside quotes for any given stock. Where most people are used to seeing a "static" quote for any given stock, a level II quote shows you the buyers and sellers within the stock and what price they are attempting to execute. This is a much more complete picture for a stock because it enables you to make your own judgments on the apparent buying or selling pressure occurring within the stock. For any person making a trade, this is extremely valuable information because it directly relates to getting in at the best price possible. Even if you were a long-term direct access trader, wouldn't you wait an extra 5 minutes if it looked like there was excessive selling pressure on the stock and it might drop significantly further, creating a better price for you to buy it at? And for day traders, this is the bread and butter of what they trade off of. A lot of times they make very quick trades by just realizing that the pressure within a stock is going to move it an eighth of a point in either direction. A level II screen also shows you the groups/institutions making the trades. This can be especially helpful if over time you are able to recognize the movements of certain market makers. In addition, you may see a certain market maker consistently selling large chunks of the stock at lower and lower prices, which is obviously another very good indicator.

Q: What are the differences among order entry and analysis software?

A: The most important thing with order entry software is that you are comfortable with using it and it provides you with all the tools you feel you need to have. Each system is a bit different, and all of them use different color-coding mechanisms and window-minimizing features, but it is most important to go with one you are comfortable with and one that has withstood the battle of the markets. By this I mean that other traders are using it and like the way it functions. Make sure to ask about other people using the software and any problems they may have had with it. Did it slow down during certain parts of the day? Has it ever crashed? What are the best and worst parts about it? Make sure to talk to more than one person because each individual uses different features of the system.

Q: How important is it to be connected to multiple ECNs?

A: It is extremely important to always have as many trading options as possible. Because each ECN acts as its own miniexchange, the more of them you have access to, the better is the chance for getting a great price. Now, once again, this matters a lot more if you are a day trader versus a long-term direct access trader, but each one is distinctly different. New ECNs are popping up all over, but there are still a few that are the ones predominantly used, such as Island and REDIbook. There is software now available, such as through Tradescape.com, that automatically routes you to all the systems. The reasons our big exchanges such as the New York Stock Exchange (NYSE) and the Nasdaq are so effective is because of the extreme levels of volume that create liquidity in the markets. If you are trading on an ECN on which there is very little volume, it can make it difficult or more time-consuming to exit positions.

Q: How do you tell if you are getting fast executions?

A: Pretty simply put, it is if your order is getting filled immediately. Having to wait in the least bit means that either your connection is too slow or maybe you are trading on an ECN that does not have enough volume. Also, it could be the system you are using to trade with, and you could ask other traders to find out if they are having the same sorts of problems.

Q: How important are such things as color coding and thermographs?

A: They are obviously important, but they do not make or break a system. Any system should use both to allow you to be able to interpret information in a more timely manner, but that is about it. It is up to each individual to decide if the system is up to par with other systems, but it should not be one of the focal points when deciding which system to use.

Q: What analytical tools does an active trader need?

A: The most important tool to a short-term direct access trader is technical analysis. Therefore, such traders really need to be able to chart stocks on any time increments in order to determine if they see any sort of patterns emerging, such as head and shoulders or support and resistance lines. They should also be able to pull up things such as volume charts to determine momentum and easily pull other histor-

ical information to analyze the information against actions that occurred in the past.

Q: How important is reliability in a system?

A: Reliability is always going to be very important. But each system
has its own little glitches from time to time. The real thing to watch
for is that your system does not become a lot slower during peak
trading times. This can really hinder your performance and take
away some of your speed advantage, which I talked about earlier. It
is always a good idea to talk to some people using the system to
get an idea of its shortfalls before you start using it. If a trader ever
tells you that the system shuts off completely from time to time, this
is clearly a red flag and something you want to avoid.

Q: How do I decide whether I should trade from home or go to an
electronic trading firm?

A: If you are going to be trading for a living, most direct access traders
find it better to work at a trading firm so that they can be around
other traders. There is an undeniable energy that surrounds all trading firms that most traders thrive off of. In addition, it enables you
to talk to other traders and find out tips and learn other things from
them. Personally, I could never trade on my own; however, I know
a lot of people who do. Some of them like to be alone because they
feel it helps them think better. If you do decide to go to a trading
firm, make sure to check the firm out before you start. The easiest
check you can do to find out about a firm is to find out if people
there are actually making money. You obviously also want to check
out the firm's systems and connections, but it is usually a good
indicator if people there are making money.

Q: How do you decide which information you should be looking at on
your screen?

A: It really goes back to using information with which you are comfortable to make your trading decisions. If you are a day trader, you
are obviously going to want to be able to have access to a lot more
charting capabilities and other technical indicators immediately accessible on your screen. If you are a long-term direct access trader,
you may be content with level II quotes and some basic fundamental

analysis such as historical charts to use in your decision making. There is so much information out there that the real issue is just getting comfortable with whatever you decide to use. Then you have to make sure that whatever system you are using to trade will allow you to quickly and easily pull up that information.

Q: What should individuals have in order to be able to day trade remotely?

A: If an individual is going to day trade remotely, there are definitely a couple of things that he or she must have. First of all, a day trader must have a computer that is not an antique and then have access to the Internet. Having DSL or some sort of faster access to the Internet instead of a 28.8-K modem is also a huge help. In addition, it is necessary to have a trading environment in which concentration is possible. Day trading in the middle of your living room with screaming kids running all around you is not ideal. Focus and concentration are absolutely critical for day traders, so you have to make sure you have the proper environment set up. It is also a good idea to get a TV on which you can have CNBC airing in the background during the course of the trading day. I even have some friends who all get together at a central location and trade there together so that they can simulate the feeling of a trading floor that much more. Many successful traders day trade from home; you just have to make sure you get everything set up so that you can trade properly over the course of a day and not be at a disadvantage compared with others at actual trading firms.

Q: What is different about what one direct access trading firm offers from another?

A: The main difference you want to be aware of is how your trades are being placed, meaning does the firm have access to all the ECNs or is it routing its trades to one particular ECN. You basically want to make sure that there is going to be a liquid enough market for you to easily buy and sell stocks. Because each ECN acts as its own miniexchange, some are obviously larger than others. What we are starting to see now, however, is that some places are routing their trades to one particular ECN, whereas others enable you to see the prices on multiple ECNs and you get to choose which one you want to execute your trade. Even some of the large brokerage firms like Charles Schwab and Goldman Sachs are investing in different ECNs so that they will be able to use them in the future.

Q: How many options are there out there for direct access traders? Will this increase or decrease?

A: New direct access trading tools are popping up every day and will only continue to increase in the future. The key is really finding established tools that others have had success with. Be leery of new products and services promising the world. The easy way to find out is to just ask successful traders what they are using. There are also a lot of new electronic trading firms opening across the country. If you are interested in trading for a living, make sure to do your homework before committing to any one firm. Once again, the easiest test is to find out how well the traders in that office are doing.

Q: What are the different options direct access traders are faced with— execution, news, analysis, software, prices, routing, etc.?

A: One of the hardest things about getting into direct access trading is deciding which tools to use. It can be pretty overwhelming when you are just getting into it. There is so much additional analysis and real-time information that it can be difficult to know where to start. The key is to remember that some individuals use lots of this information, whereas others really do not use much of it at all. Over time, you can always add new elements to your arsenal if you feel they would help you make better trades. In the beginning, however, stick to the basics.

Q: Which are the most important of each of these, and what are the bare bones of each you need to compete?

A: Well, you obviously need to be able to look at some level of historical charts. And you definitely need level II quotes. Level II quotes are definitely one of your best tools as a direct access trader. You also like to see things such as volume indicators in order to judge the momentum of the stock. Other things such as CNBC are an added bonus, but they are not absolutely necessary.

Q: What is the most important tool a direct access trader needs?

A: The most important tool is definitely level II quotes. Level II quotes enable you to see the inside bid and offer for a stock and really get a complete picture of what is happening. When you see a normal quote, you are really only seeing a snapshot of what is going on. The level II quotes enable you to gauge the way the price of the stock is heading and get in at the best price possible. A level II quote is really nothing more than an overview of all the groups trying to buy and sell a given stock at a certain price. This also ties into knowing a little bit about market makers and trying to get an understanding for their trading style within a particular stock. Because the big market makers are easy to spot, over time you will get familiar with them if you trade a particular stock on a frequent basis.

Q: What future technologies will shape direct access trading tools?

A: Direct access trading is really developing quickly. The one thing that is certain is that direct access trading is here to stay. It will just evolve and develop over time. For example, as the NYSE becomes more computerized, there obviously will be more opportunities to get involved with trading stocks listed on that exchange. Also, as international markets develop, there also will be opportunities to trade there as well. In addition, direct access trading is built on the ability to eliminate the "middleman" and get the best price possible. There is no reason why this could not apply to other securities that are readily traded on the exchanges if a market develops for them. What is definite is that direct access trading is gaining momentum very quickly, and the opportunities will only continue to multiply over the next few years. Remember, the markets are driven by liquidity, and the more people that eventually get into them, the more opportunities that will evolve.

Q: How is using the tools for direct access trading different from online investing using something like Ameritrade?

A: There are some major differences, but in the end you are really doing the same thing. As of right now, the online investing firms have a much easier-to-use interface and many "double-checking" features for their investors. Think of it as "hand-holding investing." Online firms are the "middlemen," and they hold your hand all the while you make your trade. You rely on them to get you the best price possible and to have your best interests in mind. Direct access trading is more like having a front row seat on Wall Street. You have the same tools as the Wall Street professionals and are ultimately the only one responsible for your trading. You find your own price in the market and enter and exit trades on your own terms. Although the interface is not yet as "pretty," and there is a lot more happening on your screen, it is like driving a Ferrari versus a Yugo. Another main difference is that there is no "undo" button. When you execute a trade, you are done. Therefore, it is very important to get comfortable on the keyboard. There is also access to a whole new wave of information such as level II quotes using direct access. Just remember, though, that at the end of the day, you are still buying and selling stocks. You just have a lot more power—and opportunity— by using direct access trading tools.

Q: Will this change?

A: Absolutely. In the future, direct access trading tools will become just as user-friendly as any other online investing tools. In fact, although a certain segment of the population will always use a third party to place their trades, over time the majority of individuals placing trades will do so with direct access. The big online brokerage firms know this and are getting ready to offer their customers some sort of access by investing in ECNs.

Q: What is the best way to learn how to use the direct access trading tools?

A: Far and away the best way to do it is to get on a simulator and practice. There is simply no better way. You obviously should spend some time before reading up on direct access trading and potentially talking to some other traders, but in the end, practice makes perfect. A lot of people attend seminars as well, but it is usually the same thing as reading a book. Usually the only good that can come out of it is if there are actual traders there who talk about their trading experiences. Regardless, even most traders do not know much about a lot of other trading tools out there. They know the one they use and the reasons it makes them successful. They can be one of your best sources of information.

Q: How is what happens different when you place an order on an ECN versus a traditional brokerage account?

A: When you place an order through a traditional broker, that broker is then going to its specialist on the exchange to fill the order. Therefore, your trade is handled by multiple individuals before it is actually ever executed. This can take time, as we all know, and the price is fluctuating every second. In addition, especially if you are placing your order through a traditional broker, there is no telling what other things the broker may do prior to placing your trade. It is completely out of your control. With direct access trading, you see a quantity and price available on your screen, and when you hit Enter to purchase it, you are done. You have executed the trade with another individual directly. No "middleman," nothing. You are the master of your own destiny.

Q: How did direct access trading evolve? How has the marketplace gotten to where it is right now?

A: It all started with the crash in 1987. After this crash, the Small Order Execution System (SOES) was developed as a place for private investors to be able to get out of stock without market makers backing them. This capability developed into a sort of niche for those investors who were smart enough to take advantage of it. More and more people started doing it, mostly young people who had nothing to lose and wanted to try out something new. A lot of these people— mostly the intelligent ones, the ones with competitive natures—did really, really well. This was the genesis of "day trading," which has been much in the news—both good and bad—lately. Because of the Internet, the possibility of direct access trading is now reaching more and more people, who will hopefully learn to do it in the most effective, prudent way possible.

Q: Let's say I'm an online investor and I'm working through one of the online brokers that routes trades through a specific ECN. How different is it being on just one ECN versus being connected to multiple ECNs?

A: This is a question of liquidity. If you are connected to one ECN, it follows that—because there are 10 ECNs out there—you will have a 10 percent chance of getting your order filled, at least as compared with a person connected to all 10 ECNs—thus the importance of choosing an online broker with an impartial routing system. If you are only allowed to route your orders through one specific ECN or other vehicle, it defeats the purpose of using an online broker because then you are not using any of the information—any of the liquidity—available to you through level II.

Q: How is what a direct access trading firm such as Tradescape is doing different from what other direct access trading firms or standard online brokers such as E*TRADE or Ameritrade are doing?

A: Obviously, there are many differences between different direct access trading firms, including their actual software. What Tradescape, for example, offers that some other direct access trading firms—and certainly standard online brokers—do not is years of actual level II trading experience. Sending an order to a broker who will go out and get the stock for you is level I trading. Level II trading involves driving more complicated software, back-end intelligence, logic, and functionality. That allows more in-depth information to show up on your computer screen.

Q: How can I begin learning about trading?

A: Reading good books can help you learn about trading. There are certain books, like *New Market Wizards,* that everyone reads and that can help you understand the strategy behind what goes on in the markets. Then you want to study what's going on the screen and why it happens. Trading is really about why people do what they do. As one trader says, "Your goal is to sell to people who shouldn't be buying and buy from people who shouldn't be selling. If everybody knew what they were doing, these stocks would never move."

MAJOR ECNs

Symbol	ECN Name
ARCA	Archipelago
ATTN	Attain
BRUT	Brass Securities
BTRD	Bloomberg Trade Book
CHX	Midwest Stock Exchange
INCA	Instinet
ISLD	Island
MKXT	MarketXT
NTRD	NexTrade
REDI	REDIbook by Spear, Leeds & Kellog
STRK	Strike

B

MAJOR MARKET MAKERS

Symbol	Market Maker Name
BEST	Bear, Stearns & Co., Inc.
BTAB	Alex, Brown & Sons, Inc.
GSCO	Goldman, Sachs & Co.
HMQT	Hambrecht & Quist, LLC
HRZG	Herzog, Heine, Geduld, Inc.
JANY	Janney Montgomery Scott, Inc.
LEHM	Lehman Brothers, Inc.
MADF	Bernard L. Madoff
MASH	Mayer and Schweitzer, Inc.
MLCO	Merrill Lynch, Pierce, Fenner & Smith, Inc.
MOKE	Morgan, Keehan & Co., Inc.

MONT	Nationsbanc Montgomery Securities, LLC
MSCO	Morgan Stanley & Co., Inc.
NITE	Knight Securities, L.P.
OLDE	Olde Discount Corporation
OPCO	CIBC Oppenheimer Corporation
PIPR	Piper Jaffray, Inc.
PRUS	Prudential Securities, Inc.
PWJC	Paine Webber, Inc.
RAJA	Raymond James & Associates, Inc.
SBSH	Smith Barney, Inc.
SHRP	Sharpe Capital, Inc.
SHWD	Sherwood Securities Corporation

APPENDIX C

NASDAQ SECURITIES

COMPANY (SYMBOL)	COMPANY (SYMBOL)
A	Aber Resources Ltd. (ABERF)
@plan.Inc. (APLN)	Abgenix, Inc. (ABGX)
1–800 Contacts, Inc. (CTAV)	ABIOMED, Inc. (ABMD)
1–800-FLOWERS.COM, Inc. (FLWS)	AboveNet Communications, Inc. (ABOV)
1st Bancorp (FBCV)	Accel International (ACLE)
1st Source Corporation (SRCE)	Access Anytime Bancorp, Inc. (AABC)
1st Source Corporation (SRCEP)	Access Solutions (ASICW)
1st State Bancorp, Inc. (FSBC)	Accredo Health, Inc. (ACDO)
21st Century Holding Company (TCHC)	Accrue Software, Inc. (ACRU)
24/7 Media, Inc. (TFSM)	Ace Cash Express, Inc. (AACE)
3CI Complete Compliance (TCCC)	ACMAT Corporation (ACMTA)
3D Systems Corporation (TDSC)	Acorn Holding Corp. (AVCC)
3DX Technologies, Inc. (TDXT)	Acrodyne Communications, Inc. (ACRO)
4 Kids Entertainment, Inc. (KIDE)	A.C.S. Electronics Limited (ACSEF)
4Health, Inc. (HHHHW)	Action Products International (APII)
AAON, Inc. (AAON)	Active Apparel Group, Inc. (AAGP)
ABC Bancorp (ABCB)	Active Software, Inc. (ASWX)
ABC Dispensing Technologies (ABCC)	Adams Golf, Inc. (ADGO)

COMPANY (SYMBOL)

Adaptec, Inc. (ADPT)
Adaptive Solutions, Inc. (ADSOW)
ADDvantage Media Group, Inc. (ADDM)
AdForce, Inc. (ADFC)
ADM Tronics Unlimited, Inc. (ADMT)
Admiralty Bancorp, Inc. (AAABB)
Advanced Aerodynamics & Structures, Inc. (AASI)
Advanced Environmental (AERTZ)
Advantage Bancorp, Inc. (AADV)
AEP Industries, Inc. (AEPI)
AES Corporation (The) (AESCW)
AFSALA Bancorp, Inc. (AFED)
Ag-Chem Equipment Co., Inc. (AGCH)
Agile Software Corporation (AGIL)
Agritope, Inc. (AGTOV)
Aid Auto Stores, Inc. (AIDAW)
Air Canada Corporation (ACNGF)
Aironet Wireless Communications (AIRO)
Ajay Sports, Inc. (AJAJU)
Ajay Sports, Inc. (AJAYP)
ALARIS Medical, Inc. (ALRS)
Albany Molecular Research, Inc. (AMRI)
Albion Banc Corp. (ALBC)
Alcohol Sensors International (ASIL)
Alcohol Sensors International (ASILZ)
Alexion Pharmaceuticals, Inc. (ALXN)
Allaire Corp. (ALLR)
Allegiance Telecom, Inc. (ALGX)
Allen Organ Company (AORGB)
Allergan Specialty Therapeutics, Inc. (ASTIV)
Alliance Financial Corp. (ALNC)
Alliance Resource Partners (ARLP)
Allied Holdings, Inc. (HAUL)
ALLIED Life Financial (ALFC)
Alloy Online, Inc. (ALOY)
Allscripts, Inc. (MDRX)
Allstate Financial Corporation (ASFN)
Aloette Cosmetics, Inc. (ALET)
Alpha Hospitality Corporation (ALHYW)
Alpha Industries, Inc. (ALHAA)
Alpha Microsystems (ALMI)
AlphaNet Solutions, Inc. (ALPH)
Altera Corporation (ALTR)
Alternate Postal Delivery (ALTD)
Amazon.com, Inc. (AMZN)
AMB Financial Group (AMFC)
AMBANC Corp. (AMBK)

COMPANY (SYMBOL)

AMCOL International (ACOL)
AMCON Distributing Company (DIST)
AMCOR Capital Corporation (ACAP)
Amcor Limited (AMCPF)
AMEDISYS, INC. (AMED)
AmerAlia, Inc. (AALA)
America First Apartment (APROZ)
American Aircarriers Support, Inc. (AIRS)
American Bio Medica Corp. (ABMC)
American Business Financial (ABFI)
American Champion (ACEI)
American Claims Evaluation (AMCE)
American Craft Brewing (ABREF)
American Dental Partners, Inc. (ADPI)
American Eagle Outfitters (AEOS)
American First Participating (AFPFZ)
American Growth Fund, Inc. (AGRO)
American Locker Group, Inc. (ALGI)
American National Bankshares, Inc. (AMNB)
American National Financial, Inc. (ANFI)
American Pacific Bank (AMPBB)
American Physician Partners (APPM)
American Software, Inc. (AMSWA)
American Technology Corporation (ATCO)
American United Global, Inc. (AUGIW)
American Xtai Technology, Inc. (AXTI)
AmerisSoft Corporation (AREM)
AmeriVest Properties, Inc. (AMVP)
AmerTranz Worldwide Holding (AMTZ)
AmerTranz Worldwide Holding (AMTZW)
Amgen, Inc. (AMGN)
Ampace Corporation (PACE)
Amplicon, Inc. (AMPI)
Amplidyne, Inc. (AMPDW)
AMRESCO Capital Trust (AMCT)
AMRESCO INC. (AMMB)
Amsurg Corp. (AMSGA)
Amsurg Corp. (AMSGB)
AmTrust Capital Corp. (ATSB)
ANACOMP, Inc. (ANCOW)
Andean Development Corporation (ADCC)
Andean Development Corporation (ADCCW)
Anderson Group, Inc. (ANDR)
Andyne Computing Limited (ADYNF)

COMPANY (SYMBOL)

Annuity and Life Re (Holdings), Ltd. (ALREF)
AnswerThink Consulting Group, Inc. (ANSR)
Antenna TV S.A. (ANTV)
Apollo Group Inc. Cl A (APOL)
Apollo International of Delaware (AIOD)
Apollo International of Delaware (AIODW)
Apparel Technologies, Inc. (APTXW)
Apple Computer, Inc. (AAPL)
Applied Films Corporation (AFCO)
Applied Intelligence Group (IQIQ)
Applied Materials, Inc. (AMAT)
Applied Micro Circuits (AMCC)
AppliedTheory Corp. (ATHY)
AppNet Systems, Inc. (APNT)
APS Holding Corporation (APSI)
Aqua Care Systems, Inc. (AQCRU)
Aquila Biopharmaceuticals, Inc. (AQLA)
Arbor Software Corporation (ARSW)
Area Bancshares Corporation (AREA)
Argosy Education Group, Inc. (ARGY)
Arguss Holdings, Inc. (ARGX)
ARI Network Services, Inc. (ARIS)
ARIAD Pharmaceuticals, Inc. (ARIAW)
Ariba, Inc. (ARBA)
Ariely Advertising, Limited (RELEF)
Arista Investors Corp. (ARINA)
Aristotle Corporation (The) (ARTL)
Arizona Instrument Corporation (AZIC)
Ark Restaurants Corp. (ARKR)
Arkansas Best Corporation (ABFSP)
ARM Holdings PLC (ARMY)
Arrow-Magnolia International (ARWM)
Art Technology Group, Inc. (ARTG)
Artisan Components, Inc. (ARTI)
Art's-Way Manufacturing Co. (ARTW)
ASAHI/America, Inc. (ASAM)
ASB Financial Corp. (ASBP)
Aseco Corporation (ASEC)
ASHA Corporation (ASHA)
Asia Pacific Resources, Ltd. (APQCF)
Ask Jeeves, Inc. (ASKJ)
A.S.V., Inc. (ASVI)
Aspec Technology, Inc. (ASPC)
Associated Materials Incorporated (SIDE)
Asta Funding, Inc. (ASFI)
Astro-Med, Inc. (ALOT)
Astronics Corporation (ATRO)

COMPANY (SYMBOL)

Astropower, Inc. (APWR)
Asymetrix Learning Systems, Inc. (ASYM)
At Home Corporation (ATHM)
ATC Group Services, Inc. (ATCSL)
ATEC Group Inc. (ATECW)
ATG Inc. (ATGC)
Athey Products Corporation (ATPC)
ATI Technologies Inc. (ATYTF)
Atlantic Bank and Trust (ATLB)
Atlantic Pharmaceuticals, Inc. (ATLCU)
Atlantic Preferred Capital Corp. (ATLPP)
Atlantic Realty Trust (ATLRS)
Atlas Pacific Limited (APCFY)
Atmel Corporation (ATML)
ATMI Inc. (ATMI)
ATRION Corporation (ATRI)
Auburn National (AUBN)
Audible, Inc. (ADBL)
AudioCodes Ltd. (AUDC)
Augment Systems, Inc. (AUGSW)
AutoBond Acceptance (ABND)
Autobytel.com, Inc. (ABTL)
Autologic Information (AIII)
Autoweb.com, Inc. (AWEB)
Avalon Capital, Inc. (MIST)
Avalon Community Services, (CITY)
Aviation Group, Inc. (AVGPW)
Avondale Financial Corp. (AVND)
Axsys Technologies, Inc. (AXYS)
Azurel Ltd. (AZURW)

B

Back Yard Burgers, Inc. (BYBI)
BackWeb Technologies Ltd. (BWEB)
Balance Bar Company (BBAR)
Baldwin & Lyons, Inc. (BWINA)
Baldwin & Lyons, Inc. (BWINB)
Baldwin Piano & Organ Company (BPAO)
Bally Total Fitness Holding (BFIT)
Bally's Grand, Inc. (BGLV)
Bally's Grand, Inc. (BGLVW)
Baltek Corporation (BTEK)
Baltic International USA, Inc. (BISA)
Baltic International USA, Inc. (BISAW)
bamboo.com, Inc. (BAMB)
BancFirst Corporation (BANF)
BancFirst Ohio Corp. (BFOH)
Bancinsurance Corporation (BCIS)

COMPANY (SYMBOL)

Bando McGlocklin Capital (BMCC)
Bank Corporation (The) (TBNC)
Bank of Essex (BSXT)
Bank of Granite Corporation (GRAN)
Bank of Santa Clara (BNSC)
Bank of South Carolina Corp. (BKSC)
Bank of the Ozarks (OZRK)
Bank of the Sierra (BSRR)
Bank Rhode Island (BARI)
BankAtlantic Bancorp, Inc. (BANCP)
BankFirst Corporation (BKFR)
BankUnited Financial (BKUNO)
BankUnited Financial (BKUNP)
BankUnited Financial (BKUNZ)
Banyan Strategic Realty Trust (VLANS)
Barbeques Galore Limited (BBQZY)
barnesandnoble.com, inc. (BNBN)
Base Ten Systems, Inc. (BASEB)
Batteries Batteries, Inc. (BATSW)
Bay Bancshares, Inc. (BAYB)
BCAM International Inc. (BCAML)
BCAM International Inc. (BCAMZ)
BCB Financial Services (BCBF)
BCSB Bankcorp, Inc. (BCSB)
BCT International Inc. (BCTI)
Be Incorporated (BEOS)
BeautiControl Cosmetics, Inc. (BUTI)
bebe stores, inc. (BEBE)
Bedford Bancshares, Inc. (BFSB)
Benihana Inc. (BNHN)
Benton Oil and Gas Company (BNTNW)
Beringer Wine Estates (BERW)
Berkshire Gas Company (The) (BGAS)
Bernard Haldane Associates, Inc. (BHAL)
BGS Systems, Inc. (BGSS)
B.H.I. Corporation (BHIKF)
Biacore International AB (BCOR)
Bid.Com International, Inc. (BIDS)
Big Buck Brewery & Steakhouse
  (BBUC)
Big Buck Brewery & Steakhouse
  (BBUCU)
Big Buck Brewery & Steakhouse
  (BBUCW)
Big Dog Holding, Inc. (BDOG)
Big Foot Financial Corp. (BFFC)
Big Star Entertainment, Inc. (BGST)
BindView Development Corp. (BVEW)
Bioanalytical Systems, Inc. (BASI)
Biocircuits Corporation (BIOC)

COMPANY (SYMBOL)

Biocontrol Technology, Inc. (BICO)
Bio-Imaging Technologies, Inc. (BITI)
BioMarin Pharmaceutical, Inc. (BMRN)
Biomune Systems, Inc. (BIME)
Bionutrics, Inc. (BNRX)
Biopure Corporation (BPUR)
Biora AB (BIORY)
Bio-Reference Laboratories (BRLIZ)
Biper SA de CV (BIPRY)
Bird Corporation (BIRDP)
Birmingham Utilities, Inc. (BIRM)
Birner Dental Management Services, Inc.
  (BDMS)
Biznessonline.com, Inc. (BIZZ)
BKC Semiconductors (BKCS)
Black Rock Golf Corporation (BLRK)
Block Drug Company, Inc. (BLOCA)
Blowout Entertainment, Inc. (BLWT)
Blue Dolphin Energy Company
  (BDCOD)
Blue Rhino Corporation (RINO)
BMJ Medical Management, Inc. (BONS)
BNC Mortgage, Inc. (BNCM)
Bogen Communications International
  (BOGNW)
BOK Financial Corporation (BOKF)
Bolle Inc. (BEYE)
Bonded Motors, Inc. (BMTR)
Bontex Inc. (BOTX)
Borel Bank & Trust Company (BLCA)
Boron, LePore & Associates (BLPG)
B.O.S. Better Online Solutions (BOSWF)
Boston Acoustics, Inc. (BOSA)
Boston Biomedica, Inc. (BBII)
Boston Private Bancorp, Inc. (BPBC)
Bottomline Technologies, Inc. (EPAY)
BPI Packaging Technologies (BPIEP)
Brake Headquarters U.S.A. (BHQUW)
Brass Eagle, Inc. (XTRM)
Braun Consulting, Inc. (BRNC)
Brazil Fast Food Corporation (BOBSZ)
Brazos Sportswear, Inc. (BRZS)
Brenton Banks, Inc. (BRBK)
BridgeStreet Accommodations (BEDS)
Bridgford Foods Corporation (BRID)
BrightStar Information Technology Group
  (BTSR)
Britton & Koontz Capital (BKBK)
Broadcom Corporation (BRCM)
Broadway & Seymour, Inc. (BSIS)

COMPANY (SYMBOL)

Broadway Financial Corporation (BYFC)
Brocade Communications Systems (BRCD)
Brookline Bancorp, Inc. (BRKL)
Brooks Automation, Inc. (BRKS)
Brunswick Technologies, Inc. (BTIC)
Bryn Mawr Bank Corporation (BMTC)
BT Financial Corporation (BTFC)
Buca, Inc. (BUCA)
Builders Transport (TRUKH)
Building Materials Holding (BMHC)
Bull & Bear Group, Inc. (BNBGA)
Burke Mills, Inc. (BMLS)
Business Objects S.A. (BOBJY)
BYL Bancorp (BOYL)

C

C. Brewer Homes, Inc. (CBHI)
C3, Inc. (CTHR)
Cable Michigan, Inc. (CABL)
Cade Industries, Inc. (CADE)
CAIS Internet, Inc. (CAIS)
Caliber Learning Network, Inc. (CLBR)
California Federal Bank, FSB (CALGL)
California Independent Bancorp (CIBN)
California Micro Devices (CAMD)
California Microwave, Inc. (CMICG)
California State Bank (CSTB)
Callon Petroleum Company (CLNP)
Callon Petroleum Company (CLNPP)
Calloway's Nursery, Inc. (CLWY)
Cal-Maine Foods, Inc. (CALM)
CAM Designs, Inc. (CMDAW)
Cambridge Technology Partners (CATP)
Campo Electronics, Appliances (CMPOQ)
Canandaigua Brands, Inc. (CBRNB)
Candela Corporation (CLZR)
Canisco Resources Inc. (DE) (CANR)
Cannon Express, Inc. (CANX)
Cannon Inc. (CANNY)
Cantab Pharmaceuticals PLC (CNTBY)
Cantel Industries, Inc. (CNTL)
Canterbury Information (XCEL)
Canterbury Park Holding (TRAKW)
Cape Cod Bank and Trust (CCBT)
Capital Automotive REIT (CARS)
Capital Bancorp (CBCP)
Capital Bank (CBKN)
Capital City Bank Group (CCBG)
Capital Corp of the West (CCOW)

COMPANY (SYMBOL)

Capital Environmental Resource (CERI)
Capital Factors Holding, Inc. (CAPF)
Capital Savings Bancorp, Inc. (CAPS)
Capital Southwest (CSWC)
Capitol Bancorp Ltd. (CBCL)
Capitol Federal Financial (CFFN)
CardioDynamics International (CDIC)
Cardiovascular Dynamics, Inc. (CCVD)
Career Education Corporation (CECO)
Careerbuilder, Inc. (CBDR)
CareInsite, Inc. (CARI)
Carematrix Corporation (CMDC)
Caribbean Cigar Company (CIGRW)
Caring Products International (BDRYU)
Carolina Fincorp, Inc. (CFNC)
Carolina First Bancshare, Inc. (CFBI)
Carolina Southern Bank (CSBK)
Carollton Bancorp (CRRB)
Carreker-Antinori, Inc. (CANI)
Carrier Access Corp. (CACS)
Carver Corporation (CAVR)
Casa Olé Restaurants, Inc. (CASA)
Cascade Financial Corp. (CASB)
Casco International Inc. (CASCW)
Casino Magic Corp. (CMAG)
Cass Commercial Corporation (CASS)
Castelle (CSTL)
Catapult Communications Corp. (CATT)
Cathay Bancorp, Inc. (CATY)
Cavalry Bancorp, Inc. (CAVB)
CB Bancshares, Inc. (CBBI)
CBES Bancorp, Inc. (CBES)
CBT Corporation (CBTC)
Cdnow, Inc. (CDNW)
CE Software Holdings, Inc. (CESH)
Celeritek, Inc. (CLTK)
Cellegy Pharmaceuticals, Inc. (CLGYW)
CEM Corporation (CEMX)
Centocor, Inc. (CNTO)
Central Coast Bancorp (CCBN)
Central Co-Operative Bank (CEBK)
Central Reserve Life (CRLC)
Central Virginia Bankshares (CVBK)
Centurion Mines Corporation (CTMC)
Century Bancshares, Inc. (CTRY)
Century Financial Corporation (CYFN)
CERBCO, Inc. (CERB)
Certron Corporation (CRTN)
CFC International, Inc. (CFCI)
CFS Bancorp, Inc. (CITZ)

COMPANY (SYMBOL)

CFW Communications Company (CFWC)

Chalone Wine Group, Ltd. (The) (CHLN)

Chancellor Media Corporation (ANFM)

Channell Commercial (CHNL)

Chapman Capital Management Holdings (CMGT)

Charles River Associates, Inc. (CRAI)

Charter Financial, Inc. (CBSB)

Chastain Capital Corporation (CHAS)

CHC Helicopter Corporation (FLYAF)

Cheap Tickets, Inc. (CTIX)

Chefs International, Inc. (CHEF)

Chem International, Inc. (CXILW)

Chemdex Corporation (CMDX)

Chemical Financial Corporation (CHFC)

Chemi-Trol Chemical Co. (CTRL)

Cherry Corporation (The) (CHERB)

Chester Bancorp, Inc. (CNBA)

China.com Corporation (CHINA)

Chiron Corporation (CHIR)

Chittenden Corporation (CNDN)

ChoiceTel Communications, Inc. (PHONW)

Chroma Vision Medical Systems (CVSN)

Chronimed Inc. (CHMD)

Churchill Downs, Incorporated (CHDN)

CIENA Corp. (CIEN)

Cimatron, Limited (CIMTF)

Cincinnati Financial (CINFG)

Cinemastar Luxury Theaters, (LUXYZ)

Cinram International, Inc. (CNRMF)

Cirque Energy Ltd. (CIRQF)

Citadel Communications Corp. (CITC)

Citizens Bancshares, Inc. (CICS)

Citizens Financial Corporation (CNFL)

CNBT Bancshares, Inc. (CNBT)

Citrix Systems, Inc. (CTXS)

City Holding Company Trust II (CHCOP)

CKF Bancorp, Inc. (CKFB)

Claimsnet.com, Inc. (CLAI)

Clarent Corporation (CLRN)

Clark/Bardes Holdings, Inc. (CLKB)

Classic Bancshares, Inc. (CLAS)

Clayton Williams Energy, Inc. (CWEI)

Clean Diesel Technologies, Inc. (CDTI)

Clean Harbors, Inc. (CLHB)

Cleveland Indians Baseball Company, Inc. (CLEV)

CleveTrust Realty Investors (CTRIS)

COMPANY (SYMBOL)

ClinTrials Research Inc. (CCRO)

CMGI, Inc. (CMGI)

CNB Financial Corporation (CCNE)

CNET, Inc. (CNET)

CNS Bancorp, Inc. (CNSB)

CNY Financial Corporation (CBIC)

Coast Bancorp (CTBP)

Coast Federal Litigation Contingent Payment (CCPRZ)

Cobalt Group, Inc. (The) (CBLT)

CoBancorp, Inc. (COBI)

Coda Music Technology, Inc. (COMT)

Coflexip (CXIPY)

Cognicase Inc. (COGIF)

Cognizant Technology Solutions Corporation (CTSH)

Cohesant Technologies Inc. (COHT)

Cohoes Bancorp, Incorporated (COHB)

Coinmach Laundry Corporation (WDRY)

CollaGenex Pharmaceuticals (CGPI)

Collateral Therapeutics, Inc. (CLTX)

Colonial Commercial Corp. (CCOM)

Colonial Commercial Corp. (CCOMP)

Colony Bankcorp, Inc. (CBAN)

Colorado Business Bankshares, Inc. (COBZ)

Columbia Bancorp (CBBO)

Columbia Bancorp (CBMD)

Columbia Banking System, Inc. (COLB)

Columbia Financial of Kentucky, Inc. (CFKY)

Columbia Sportswear Company (COLM)

Columbus McKinnon Corporation (CMCO)

Com21, Inc. (CMTO)

Comair Holdings, Inc. (COMR)

CombiChem, Inc. (CCHM)

Comm Bancorp, Inc. (CCBP)

Command Systems, Inc. (CMND)

Commander Aircraft Company (CMDR)

Commerce Bank/Harrisburg (COBH)

Commerce One, Inc. (CMRC)

Commercial Bank of New York (CBNY)

Commercial National Financial (CNAF)

Commonwealth Bancorp, Inc. (CMSB)

Commtouch Software Ltd. (CTCH)

Communications World (CWII)

Community Bank Shares of Indiana (CBIN)

Community Financial Holding (CMFH)

COMPANY (SYMBOL)

Community First Banking (CFBC)
Community Medical Transport (CMTI)
Community Savings Bancshares (CMSV)
Community Trust Bancorp, Inc. (CTBI)
Community Trust Bancorp, Inc. (CTBIP)
Community West Bancshares (GLTB)
COMPS.COM, Inc. (CDOT)
CompScript Inc. (CPRX)
CompuCredit Corporation (CCRT)
CompuDyne Corporation (CDCY)
CompuMed, Inc. (CMPD)
Computer Language Research (CLRI)
Computer Literacy, Inc. (CMPL)
Computone Corporation (CMPT)
Comtrex Systems Corporation (COMX)
Comverse Technology, Inc. (CMVT)
Concepts Direct, Inc. (CDIR)
Concur Technologies, Inc. (CNQR)
Condor Technology Solutions, Inc.
   (CNDR)
Conductus, Inc. (CDTS)
Conexant Systems, Inc. (CNXT)
CONMED Corporation (CNMD)
Conning Corporation (CNNG)
Conrad Industries, Inc. (CNRD)
Consolidated Mercantile Corp. (CSLMF)
Consulier Engineering, Inc. (CSLR)
Consumers Financial (CFINP)
Continental Choice Care, Inc. (CCCI)
Continental Health Affiliates (CTHL)
Continental Information (CISC)
Continental Mortgage (CMETS)
Continental Natural Gas, Inc. (CNGL)
Continuous Software Corp. (CNSW)
Contour Medical, Inc. (CTMI)
Control Chief Holdings, Inc. (DIGM)
Convergent Communications, Inc.
   (CONV)
Conversion Technologies (CTIXW)
Cooperative Bankshares, Inc. (COOP)
Copper Mountain Networks, Inc.
   (CMTN)
CoreComm Limited (BKFRF)
Corinthian Colleges, Inc. (COCO)
Corixa Corporation (CRXA)
Corporate Executive Board Company
   (EXBD)
Corporate Office Properties (RLIN)
Corporate Renaissance Group, Inc.
   (CREN)

COMPANY (SYMBOL)

Correctional Services (CSCQ)
Cortech, Inc. (CRTQ)
Cortecs PLC (DLVRY)
CORUS Bankshares, Inc. (CORS)
CorVel Corporation (CRVL)
Cosmetic Center, Inc. (The) (COSC)
Cost-U-Less, Inc. (CULS)
Cotton States Life Insurance (CSLI)
Covad Communications Group, Inc.
   (COVD)
Covalent Group, Inc. (CVGR)
Covenant Bancorp, Inc. (CNSK)
Covenant Bancorp, Inc. (CNSKO)
Covenant Transport, Inc. (CVTI)
CoVest Bancshares, Inc. (COVB)
Covol Technologies, Inc. (CVOL)
Cowlitz Bancorporation (CWLZ)
Coyote Network Systems, Inc. (CYOE)
CPAC, Inc. (CPAK)
CPB, Inc. (CPBI)
Cragar Industries, Inc. (CRGRW)
Crazy Woman Creek Bancorp (CRZY)
Creative Host Services, Inc. (CHST)
Creative Master International, Inc.
   (CMST)
Credit Depot Corporation (LEND)
Creditrust Corp. (CRDT)
Credo Petroleum Corporation (CRED)
Creo Products, Inc. (CREOV)
Crescendo Pharmaceuticals (CNDO)
Crescent Operating, Inc. (COPI)
Cresud S.A.C.I.F. y A. (CRESY)
CRH, public limited company (CRHCY)
Critical Path, Inc. (CPTH)
Cronos Group (The) (CRNSF)
Crown Andersen Inc. (CRAN)
Crown Castle International Corp. (TWRS)
Crusader Holding Corp. (CRSB)
Cryomedical Sciences, Inc. (CMSI)
Crystal Systems Solutions (CRYSF)
CSK Corporation (CSKKY)
CTB International Corp. (CTBC)
CTI Industries Corporation (CTIB)
CulturalAccess Worldwide, Inc. (CAWW)
Cumberland Technologies, Inc. (CUMB)
Cumulus Media, Inc. (CMLS)
Cunningham Graphics International, Inc.
   (CGII)
CuraGen Corporation (CRGN)
Curtis International Ltd. (CURTF)

COMPANY (SYMBOL)

Cusac Gold Mines, Limited (CUSWF)
Cutco Industries, Inc. (CUTC)
CyBear, Inc. (CYBA)
Cyberian Outpost, Inc. (COOL)
CyberSource Corporation (CYBS)
Cytoclonal Pharmaceutics Inc. (CYPH)

D

D & E Communications, Inc. (DECC)
D. G. Jewellery of Canada Ltd. (DGJLF)
D. G. Jewellery of Canada Ltd. (DGJWF)
DA Consulting Group, Inc. (DACG)
Dai'ei, Inc. (DAIEY)
Dakotah, Incorporated (DKTH)
Daktronics, Inc. (DAKT)
Daniel Green Company (DAGR)
Dart Group Corporation (DARTA)
Data Translation Inc. (DATX)
Datalink Corporation (DTLK)
Datamark Holding, Inc. (DTAM)
Datum, Inc. (DATM)
Davel Communications Group (DAVL)
David's Bridal, Inc. (DABR)
Deb Shops, Inc. (DEBS)
Decoma International, Inc. (DECF)
DECS Trust V (TWDE)
Dell Computer Corporation (DELL)
Delta Petroleum Corporation (DPTR)
Delta-Galil Industries Ltd. (DELT)
Deltek Systems, Inc. (DLTK)
Denali Incorporated (DNLI)
Dental/Medical Diagnostic (DMDS)
Dental/Medical Diagnostic (DMDSW)
DENTSPLY International Inc. (XRAY)
DepoMed, Inc. (DPMD)
DepoMed, Inc. (DPMDW)
Descartes Systems Group Inc. (DSGXF)
Desert Community Bank (DCBK)
Designs, Inc. (DESI)
Destia Communications, Inc. (DEST)
DHB Capital Group (DHBT)
dick clark productions, inc. (DCPI)
Didax, Inc. (AMEN)
Diehl Graphsoft, Inc. (DIEG)
Digex, Inc. (DIGX)
Digital Island, Inc. (ISLD)
Digital Recorders, Inc. (TBUS)
Digital River, Inc. (DRIV)
Digital Transmission Systems (DTSXW)
Digitale Telekabel AG (DTAGY)

COMPANY (SYMBOL)

Diplomat Corporation (DIPLW)
Direct Focus, Inc. (DFXI)
Disc Graphics, Inc. (DSGR)
Disc Graphics, Inc. (DSGRW)
Discovery Laboratories Inc. (DSCOU)
Discovery Laboratories Inc. (DSCOW)
Ditech Communications Corp. (DITC)
DLB Oil & Gas, Inc. (DLBI)
DNAP Holding Corporation (DNAP)
DOCdata N.V. (DOCDF)
DocuCorp International, Inc. (DOCCR)
Dollar Tree Stores, Inc. (DLTR)
Dominguez Services Corporation
  (DOMZ)
Donegal Group, Inc. (DGIC)
Doral Financial Corp. (DORLP)
Dorel Industries, Inc. (DIIBF)
Double Eagle Petroleum and Mining Co.
  (DBLE)
Double Eagle Petroleum and Mining Co.
  (DBLEW)
DoubleClick, Inc. (DCLK)
drkoop.com, Inc. (KOOP)
Drug Emporium, Inc. (DEMPG)
Drugstore.com, Inc. (DSCM)
DSET Corporation (DSET)
DSG International Limited (DSGIF)
DT Industries, Inc. (DTII)
DTM Corporation (DTMC)
Dura Pharmaceuticals, Inc. (DURAH)
Dyna Group International, Inc. (DGIX)
DynaGen, Inc. (CYGNW)
Dynamic Oil Limited (DYOLF)
Dynamics Research Corporation (DRCO)
Dynatec International, Inc. (DYNX)
Dynex Capital Inc. (DXCPO)
Dynex Capital Inc. (DXCPP)

E

Eagle BancGroup, Inc. (EGLB)
EarthCare Company (ECCO)
EarthShell Container Corporation (ERTH)
EarthWeb Inc. (EWBX)
East West Bancorp, Inc. (EWBC)
Eastco Industrial Safety Corp. (ESTOW)
Eastco Industrial Safety Corp. (ESTOZ)
eBay, Inc. (EVAY)
Echelon Corp. (ELON)
EchoCath, Inc. (ECHTA)
EchoStar Communications (DISHP)

COMPANY (SYMBOL)

Eclipsys Corporation (ECLP)
Ecomat, Inc. (ECMT)
EcoScience Corporation (ECSC)
EcoTyre Technologies, Inc. (ETTIW)
Edac Technologies Corporation (EDAC)
Edelbrock Corporation (EDEL)
Edgar Online, Inc. (EDGR)
Edison Control Corporation (EDCO)
Education Management (EDMC)
Educational Insights, Inc. (EDIN)
Effective Management Systems (EMSI)
Effective Management Systems (EMSIW)
Efficient Networks, Inc. (EFNT)
EFI Electronics Corporation (EFIC)
EFTC Corporation (EFTC)
Elder-Beerman Stores Corp. (The)
    (EBSCV)
Electronic Boutique Holdings Corp.
    (ELBO)
Electronic Designs, Inc. (EDIXW)
Electronica Tele-Communications
    (ETCIA)
Electro-Sensors, Inc. (ELSE)
Elmer's Restaurants, Inc. (ELMS)
Elmira Savings Bank, FSB (The) (ESBK)
E-Loan, Inc. (EELN)
ELXSI Corporation (ELXS)
EMC Insurance Group, Inc. (EMCI)
EMCEE Broadcast Products (ECIN)
EMCORE Corporation (EMKR)
Emerald Isle Bancorp, Inc. (EIRE)
Emons Transporation Group (EMON)
Empire Federal Bancorp, Inc. (EFBC)
Encore Wire Corporation (WIRE)
Energy Search, Incorporated (EGAS)
Energy Search, Incorporated (EGASW)
Energy West, Inc. (EWST)
e-Net, Inc. (ETELW)
Enex Resources Corporation (ENEX)
Engage Technologies, Inc. (ENGA)
Engel General Developers Ltd. (ENGEF)
Engineering Measurements (EMCO)
Enhanced Services Company (ESVS)
Ensec International, Inc. (ENSC)
ENStar, Inc. (ENSR)
Entrust Technologies, Inc. (ENTU)
Envirodyne Industries, Inc. (EDYN)
Envirogen, Inc. (ENVGU)
Enzon, Inc. (ENZN)
Equitable Federal Savings Bank (EQSB)

COMPANY (SYMBOL)

Equity Marketing, Inc. (EMAK)
ErgoBilt, Inc. (ERGB)
ESELCO, Inc. (EDSE)
Eskimo Pie Corporation (EPIE)
ESPS, Inc. (ESPS)
Esquire Communications Ltd. (ESQSW)
E-Tek Dynamics, Inc. (ETEK)
eToys, Inc. (ETYS)
Euro Tech Holdings Company (CLWWF)
Europa Cruises Corporation (KRUZ)
European Micro Holdings, Inc. (EMCC)
Evans & Sutherland Computer (ESCC)
Evans & Sutherland Computer (ESCCG)
Evans, Inc. (EVAN)
Evans Systems, Inc. (EVSI)
Evolving Systems, Inc. (EVOL)
Excalibur Technologies (EXCA)
Excel Switching Corporation (XLSW)
Excel Technology, Inc. (XLTC)
Exchange Applications, Inc. (EXAP)
Executive TeleCard, Ltd. (EXTL)
EXECUTONE Information Systems
    (XTON)
Exigent International, Inc. (XGNT)
Exodus Communications, Inc. (EXDS)
Expeditors International of Washington,
    Inc. (EXPD)
Extended Systems Incorporated (XTND)
Extreme Networks, Inc. (EXTR)
Ezcony Interamerica Inc. (EZCOF)

F

F & M Bancorp (FMBN)
F & M Bancorporation, Inc. (FMBK)
F5 Networks, Inc. (FFIV)
Failure Group, Inc. (The) (FAIL)
Fantom Technologies Inc. (FTMTF)
Farmer Brothers Company (FARM)
Farmers Capital Bank (FFKT)
Farr Company (FARC)
Farrel Corporation (FARL)
Fashionmall.com, Inc. (FASH)
FCNB Corporate Trust (FCNBP)
Featherlite Mg., Inc. (FTHR)
Federal Screw Works (FSCR)
FFD Financial Corporation (FFDF)
FFLC Bancorp, Inc. (FFLC)
FFVA Financial Corporation (FFFC)
FFW Corporation (FFWC)
Fiberstars, Inc. (FBST)

COMPANY (SYMBOL)

Fidelity Bancorp, Inc. (FSBI)
Fidelity Financial of Ohio (FFOH)
Fidelity Holdings, Inc. (FDHG)
Fieldcrest Cannon, Inc. (FLDCP)
Fields Aircraft Spares, Inc. (FASI)
Financial Industries (FNIN)
Financial Institutions, Inc. (FISI)
FinishMaster, Inc. (FMST)
First Albany Companies, Inc. (FACT)
First Bancorp of Indiana, Inc. (FBEI)
First Banks, Inc. (FBNKO)
First Bell Bancorp, Inc. (FBBC)
First Charter Corporation (FCTR)
First Coastal Corporation (FCME)
First Colonial Group, Inc. (FTCG)
First Commerce Bancshares (FCBIA)
First Community Financial Corp. (FCFN)
First Consulting Group, Inc. (FCGI)
First Corporation of Long Island (FLIC)
First Dynasty Mines Ltd. (FDYMF)
First Enterprise Financial (FENT)
First Federal Bancorp, Inc. (FFBZ)
First Federal Bancorporation (BDJI)
First Federal Capital Corp. (FTFC)
First Federal Savings and Loan (FFES)
First Financial Bancorp. (FFBC)
First Financial Bancorp, Inc. (FFBI)
First Financial Bankshares (FFIN)
First Financial Corp. (FTFN)
First Home Bancorp, Inc. (FSPG)
First Kansas Financial Corporation
    (FKAN)
First Keystone Financial, Inc. (FKFS)
First Liberty Financial Corp. (FLFC)
First Mariner Bancorp (FMAR)
First Merchants Corporation (FRME)
First Midwest Financial, Inc. (CASH)
First Mutual Savings Bank (FMSB)
First National Lincoln Corp. (FNLC)
First Northern Capital (FNGB)
First Oak Brook Bancshares (FOBBA)
First Place Financial Corporation (FPFC)
First Savings Bancorp Inc. (SOPN)
First South Africa Corp., Ltd. (FSAUF)
First Southern Bancshares, Inc. (FSTH)
First Sterling Banks, Inc. (FSLB)
First United Bancorporation (FUSC)
First United Bancshares, Inc. (UNTD)
First United Capital Trust (FUNCP)

COMPANY (SYMBOL)

First United Corporation (FUNC)
First Victoria National Bank (FVNB)
First Virtual Corporation (FVCX)
First Years, Inc. (The) (KIDD)
Firstar Corporation (FSRPZ)
FirstBank Corp. (FBNW)
Firstbank of Illinois Co. (FBIC)
FirstCity Financial (FCFCP)
FirstFed Bancorp, Inc. (FFDB)
FirstFederal Financial (FFSWO)
Firstmark Corp. (FIRM)
Flagstar Bancorp, Inc. (FLGSP)
Flamemaster Corporation (The) (FAME)
FlashNet Communications, Inc. (FLAS)
Fletcher's Fine Foods Ltd. (FLCHF)
FlexiInternational Software (FLXI)
Flexsteel Industries, Inc. (FLXS)
Florida Banks, Inc. (FLBK)
Florida Gaming Corporation (BETS)
FloridaFirst Bancorp (FFBK)
Florsheim Group Inc. (FLSC)
Fluor Daniel GTI, Inc. (FDGT)
Flycast Communications Corp. (FCST)
FMS Financial Corporation (FMCO)
F.N.B. Corporation (FBAN)
F.N.B. Corporation (FBANP)
FNB Corp. (FNBN)
FNB Corporation (FNBP)
FNB Financial Services (FNBF)
Focal Communications Corp. (FCOM)
Foilmark, Inc. (FLMK)
Food Court Entertainment (FCENA)
Food Court Entertainment (FCENZ)
Food Technology Service, Inc. (VIFL)
Foothill Independent Bancorp (FOOT)
For Better Living, Inc. (FBTR)
Formula Systems (1985) Ltd. (FORTY)
Fort Thomas Financial (FTSB)
FP Bancorp Inc. (FPBN)
Franklin Bank, National (FSVB)
Franklin Electric Co., Inc. (FELE)
Freeserve PLC (FREE)
Frontier Natural Gas (FNGC)
Frontier Natural Gas (FNGCP)
Frontier Natural Gas (FNGCW)
FRP Properties, Inc. (FRPP)
Fulton Financial Corporation (FULT)
Fundtech, Ltd. (FNDTF)
Fusion Systems Corporation (FUSNR)

COMPANY (SYMBOL)

G

G. Willi-Food International (WILCF)
G. Willi-Food International (WILWF)
Gadzoox Networks, Inc. (ZOOX)
Gaston Federal Bancorp, Inc. (GBNK)
GB&T Bancshares, Inc. (GBTB)
General Binding Corporation (GBND)
Genesee & Wyoming Inc. (GNWR)
Genesee Corporation (GENBB)
Genesis Direct, Inc. (GEND)
Genesis Microchip, Inc. (GNSSF)
GenesisIntermedia.com, Inc. (GENI)
Genisys Reservation Systems (GENSW)
Genisys Reservation Systems (GENSZ)
Genta Incorporated (GNTA)
Genzyme Molecular Oncology (GZMO)
GeoResources, Inc. (GEOI)
George Mason Bankshares, Inc. (GMBS)
Gerald Stevens, Inc. (GIFT)
German American Bancorp. (GABC)
GFS Bancorp, Inc. (GFSB)
Giant Cement Holding, Inc. (GCHI)
Gibbs Construction, Inc. (GBSEW)
Giga Information Group, Inc. (GIGX)
Gilman & Ciocia, Inc. (GTAXW)
Gish Biomedical, Inc. (GISH)
GKN Holding Corp. (GKNS)
Glacier Bancorp, Inc. (GBCI)
Glassmaster Company (GLMA)
Global Crossing Ltd. (GBLX)
Global Imaging Systems, Inc. (GISX)
Global Intellicom, Inc. (GBIT)
Global Med Technologies, Inc. (GLOB)
Global Pharmaceutical (GLPC)
Global Sports, Inc. (GSPT)
Global TeleSystems Group, Inc. (GTSG)
GlobeSpan, Inc. (GSPN)
Gold Banc Corporation, Inc. (GLDB)
Gold Fields of South Africa (GLDFY)
Golden Eagle Group, Inc. (GEGPW)
Golden Isles Financial (GIFHU)
Golden State Vintners, Inc. (VINT)
Golf Training Systems, Inc. (GTSX)
Good Times Restaurants Inc. (GTIM)
GoodNoise Corporation (EMUS)
Goran Capital, Inc. (GNCNF)
GoTo.com, Inc. (GOTO)
Gradco Systems, Inc. (GRCO)
Grand Court Lifestyles, Inc. (GCLI)

COMPANY (SYMBOL)

Granite Broadcasting (GBTVP)
Granite Financial, Inc. (GFNI)
Granite State Bankshares, Inc. (GSBI)
Grease Monkey Holding (GMHC)
Great American Bancorp, Inc. (GTPS)
Great Bee Dee Bancorp, Inc. (PEDE)
Great Central Mines Ltd. (GTCMY)
Great Pee Dee Bancorp, Inc. (PEDE)
Greater Atlantic Financial Corp. (GAFC)
Greater Bay Bancorp (GBBK)
Greater Bay Bancorp (GBBKP)
Greater Community Bancorp (GFLSP)
Green Mountain Coffee, Inc. (GMCR)
Greene County Bancorp. Inc. (GCBC)
Greenstone Roberts (GRRI)
Greif Bros. Corporation (GBCOA)
Griffin Land & Nurseries, Inc. (GRIF)
Grist Mill Co. (GRST)
GSB Financial Corporation (GOSB)
GST Telecommunications (GSTX)
Guaranty Bancshares, Inc. (GNTY)
Guaranty Financial Corporation (GSLC)
Gulf West Banks, Inc. (GWBK)
Gyrodyne Company of America (GYRO)
GZA GeoEnvironmental (GZEA)

H

H. D. Vest, Inc. (HDVS)
Habersham Bancorp (HABC)
Hahn Automotive Warehouse (HAHN)
Hampshire Group, Limited (HAMP)
Hanover Gold Company, Inc. (HYGO)
Happy Kids, Inc. (HKID)
Harbor Federal Bancorp, Inc. (HRBF)
Hardin Bancorp, Inc. (HFSA)
Hardinge, Inc. (HDNG)
Harleysville National (HNBC)
Harmon Industries, Inc. (HRMN)
Harmony Brook, Inc. (HBRK)
Harrington Financial Group (HFGI)
Harrodsburg First Financial (HFFB)
Harvard Industries, Inc. (HAVAV)
Harvest Restaurant Group, Inc. (ROTIZ)
Hastings Entertainment, Inc. (HAST)
Hathaway Corporation (HATH)
Haverty Furniture Companies (HAVTA)
Hawaiian Natural Water (HNWC)
Hawaiian Natural Water (HNWCU)
Hawker Pacific Aerospace (HPAC)

COMPANY (SYMBOL)

Hawkins Chemical, Inc. (HWKN)
Hayes Corporation (HAYZ)
HCB Bancshares, Inc. (HCBB)
HeadHunter.NET, Inc. (HHNT)
Health Systems Design (HSDC)
Healtheon Corp. (HLTH)
HealthRite Inc. (HLRT)
Hechinger Company (HECHH)
Hector Communications (HCCO)
Hector Communications (HCCOG)
Heidrick & Struggles International (HSII)
Helisys, Inc. (HELI)
Help At Home, Inc. (HAHI)
Hemagen Diagnostics, Inc. (HMGN)
Hemlock Federal Financial (HMLK)
Henley Healthcare, Inc. (HENL)
Heritage Bancorp, Inc. (HBCI)
Heritage Financial Corporation (HFWA)
Herley Industries, Inc. (HRLYW)
Hertz Technology Group, Inc. (HERZ)
Herzfeld Caribbean Basin Fund (CUBA)
Heuristic Development Group (IFIT)
Heuristic Development Group (IFITU)
Heuristic Development Group (IFITW)
Heuristic Development Group (IFITZ)
HF Financial Corp. (HFFC)
Hibernia Foods Public Limited (HIBWF)
Hickok Incorporated (HICKA)
Hickory Tech Corporation (HTCO)
hi/fn, inc. (HIFN)
High Country Bancorp, Inc. (HCBC)
High Speed Access Corporation (HSAC)
Highland Bancorp, Inc. (HBNK)
Highway Holdings Limited (HIHWF)
Highwood Resources Ltd. (HIWDF)
Hines Horticulture, Inc. (HORT)
Hirel Holdings, Inc. (HIRL)
HLM Design, Inc. (HLMD)
HMT Technology Corporation (HMTTG)
Holiday RV Superstores, Inc. (RVEE)
Hollinger Inc. (HLGUF)
Holt's Cigar Holdings, Inc. (HOLT)
Home Bancorp (HBFW)
Home Building Bancorp, Inc. (HBBI)
Home Centers (DIY), Limited (HOMEF)
Home Loan Financial Corporation
   (HLFC)
HomeCorp, Inc. (HMCI)
homestore.com, Inc. (HOMS)
Hometown Auto Retailers, Inc. (HCAR)

COMPANY (SYMBOL)

Hoover's, Inc. (HOOV)
HopFed Bancorp, Inc. (HFBC)
Horizon Bancorp, Inc. (HZWV)
Horizon Medical Products, Inc. (HMPS)
Horizon Offshore, Inc. (HOFF)
Horizon Organic Holding Corp. (HCOW)
Hotel Discovery, Inc. (HOTDU)
Hotel Discovery, Inc. (HOTDW)
HotJobs.com, Ltd. (HOTJ)
Howell Corporation (HWLLP)
Hudson City Bancorp, Inc. (HCBK)
Hudson Hotels Corporation (HUDS)
Hudson River Bancorp, Inc. (HRBT)
Hungarian Broadcasting Corp. (HBCOP)
Hyde Athletic Industries, Inc. (HYDEA)
HyperMedia Communications (HYPR)

I

I V C Industries, Inc. (IVCO)
I.D. Systems, Inc. (IDSY)
ICHOR Corporation (ICHR)
ICO Global Communications, Limited
   (ICOGF)
ICON PLC (ICLRY)
IDG Books Worldwide, Inc. (IDGB)
IIC Industries Inc. (IICR)
IL Foranio (America) (ILFO)
Image Sensing Systems, Inc. (ISNS)
Image Systems Corporation (IMSG)
ImageX.com, Inc. (IMGX)
Imark Technologies, Inc. (MAXXW)
ImmuCell Corporation (ICCC)
ImmuLogic Pharmaceutical (IMUL)
Immunex Corporation (IMNX)
Imtec, Inc. (IMTC)
Independence Brewing Company (IBCO)
Independence Community Bank Corp.
   (ICBC)
Independence Federal Savings (IFSB)
Independent Bank Corporation (IBCP)
Independent Energy Holdings PLC
   (INDYY)
Indiana Community Bank, SB (INCB)
Indiana United Bancorp (IUBCP)
Indigo Aviation AB (IAABY)
Industrial Acoustics Company (IACI)
Industrial Bancorp, Inc. (INBI)
Industrial Holdings, Inc. (IHIIL)
Industrial Holdings, Inc. (IHIIZ)
Industrial Services of America (IDSA)

COMPANY (SYMBOL)

Indusri-Matematik (IMIC)
Inet Technologies, Inc. (INTI)
Infinite Machines Corp. (IMCIW)
InfoCure Corp. (INCX)
Informatica Corporation (INFA)
Information Management (IMAA)
Infosafe Systems, Inc. (ISFEU)
Infosafe Systems, Inc. (ISFEW)
InfoSpace.com, Inc. (INSP)
Infosys Technologies Limited (INFY)
Initio, Inc. (INTO)
Inkine Pharmaceutical Company
  (INKPW)
Inktomi Corporation (INKT)
Inland Casino Corporation (INLD)
Inmark Enterprises, Inc. (IMKE)
InnoPet Brands Corp. (INBC)
InnoPet Brands Corp. (INBCW)
InnoServ Technologies Inc. (ISER)
Innotrac Corporation (INOC)
INSCI Corporation (INSIW)
Insight Communications Company (ICCI)
Insilco Corporation (INSL)
Insituform East, Incorporated (INEI)
Instrumentarium Corporation (INMRY)
Insurance Management Solutions Group
  (INMG)
InsWeb Corporation (INSW)
Integral Systems, Inc. (ISYS)
Integrated Measurement (IMSC)
Integrated Systems Consulting (ISCG)
Intellicall, Inc. (ICL)
Intellicell Corp. (FONE)
Intelligent Life Corporation (ILIF)
Intensiva HealthCare (IHCC)
Interactive Magic, Inc. (IMGK)
Interactive Pictures Corporation (IPIX)
InterCept Group, Inc. (The) (ICPT)
Intercontinental Life (ILCO)
Intergroup Corporation (The) (INTG)
Interliant, Inc. (INIT)
International Aircraft (IAIS)
International Assets Holding (IAAC)
International Bancshares Corp. (IBOC)
International Integration, Inc. (ICUB)
International Microcomputer (IMSI)
International Nursing Services (NURS)
International Sports (ISWI)
International Sports (ISWIW)
Internet America, Inc. (GEEK)

COMPANY (SYMBOL)

Internet Capital Group (ICGE)
Internet Gold (IGLD)
internet.com LLC (INTM)
Interplay Entertainment Corporation
  (IPLY)
Interstate National Dealer (ISTN)
Intervisual Books, Inc. (IVBK)
InterWest Bancorp Inc. (IWBK)
Interwest Home Medical, Inc. (IWHM)
InterWorld Corporation (INTW)
InTime Systems International (TAMSA)
InTime Systems International (TAMSW)
Intraware, Inc. (ITRA)
Investors Real Estate Trust (IRETS)
Invitrogen Corporation (IVGN)
Ionic Fuel Technology, Inc. (IFTIW)
Ionic Fuel Technology, Inc. (IFTIZ)
IPL Energy Inc. (IPPIF)
Ipswich Savings Bank (IPSW)
IRATA, Inc. (IRATW)
Iroquois Bancorp, Inc. (IROQ)
Irwin Financial Corporation (IRWNP)
I.S.G. Technologies, Inc. (ISGTF)
Israel Land Development (ILDCY)
Isramco, Inc. (ISRLZ)
ISS Group, Inc. (ISSX)
iTurf, Inc. (TURF)
iVillage Inc. (IVIL)
IWL Communications (IWLC)
iXL Enterprises, Inc. (IIXL)
Ixnet, Inc. (EXNT)
IXOS Software AG (XOSY)

J

J2 Communications (JTWOW)
Jacksonville Bancorp, Inc. (JXVL)
Jacksonville Savings Bank (JXSB)
Jacobson Stores Inc. (JCBSG)
Jacor Communications, Inc. (JCORL)
Jacor Communications, Inc. (JCORM)
Jannock Limited (JANNF)
Japan Air Lines Company, Ltd. (JAPNY)
Jason Incorporated (JASN)
Javelin Systems, Inc. (JVLN)
JB Oxford Holdings, Inc. (JBOH)
Jean Philippe Fragrances, Inc. (JEAN)
JeffBanks, Inc. (JEFF)
JeffBanks, Inc. (JEFFP)
Jenkon International, Inc. (JNKN)
Jenna Lane, Inc. (JLNY)

COMPANY (SYMBOL)

JetForm Corporation (FORMF)
JFAX.COM, Inc. (JFAX)
JG Industries, Inc. (JGIN)
JLM Industries, Inc. (JLMI)
JMAR Industries, Inc. (JMARU)
JMAR Industries, Inc. (JMARW)
Joachim Bancorp, Inc. (JOAC)
John B. Sanfilippo & Son, Inc. (JBSS)
Johnson Worldwide Associates (JWAIA)
Jones Intercable, Inc. (JOIN)
JPS Textile Group, Inc. (JPST)
Juniper Networks, Inc. (JNPR)
Juno Online Services, Inc. (JWEB)

K

K2 Design, Inc. (KTWO)
K2 Design, Inc. (KTWOW)
Kaiser Ventures, Inc. (KRSC)
Kaman Corporation (KAMNG)
Karts International (KINTW)
Kaye Group, Inc. (KAYE)
Keith Companies, Inc. (The) (TKCI)
Kenan Transport Company (KTCO)
Kendle International Inc. (KNDL)
Kent Financial Services, Inc. (KENT)
Kentucky Electric Steel, Inc. (KESI)
Kevco, Inc. (KVCO)
Kewaunee Scientific (KEQU)
Key Florida Bancorp, Inc. (KEYB)
King Pharmaceuticals, Inc. (KING)
Kinnard Investments, Inc. (KINN)
KLLM Transport Services, Inc. (KLLM)
Knape & Vogt Manufacturing (KNAP)
Knight/Trimark Group, Inc. (NITE)
Koala Corporation (KARE)
Koss Corporation (KOSS)
KS Bancorp, Inc. (KSAV)
KSB Bancorp, Inc. (KSBK)
K-Tron International, Inc. (KTII)
KWG Resources, Inc. (KWGDF)
Kyzen Corporation (KYZNW)

L

L. B. Foster Company (FSTRA)
Lab Holdings, Inc. (LABH)
LaCrosse Footwear, Inc. (BOOT)
Ladish Company (LDSH)
Lady Luck Gaming Corporation (LUCK)
LaJolla Pharmaceutical Company (LJPC)
Lake Ariel Bancorp, Inc. (LABN)

COMPANY (SYMBOL)

Lakeland Financial Corporation (LKFN)
Lakeland Financial Corporation (LKFNP)
Lakeland Industries, Inc. (LAKE)
Lakes Gaming, Inc. (LACO)
Lam Research Corporation (LRCX)
Lamar Capital Corporation (LCCO)
Laminating Technologies, Inc. (LAMT)
Laminating Technologies, Inc. (LAMTU)
Lancaster Colony Corporation (LANC)
Lancit Media Entertainment Ltd. (LNCT)
Landmark Bancshares, Inc. (LARK)
Langer Biomechanics Group (GAIT)
Las Vegas Entertainment (LVENZ)
Laser Corporation (LSER)
Laser Power Corporation (LPWR)
Latin American Casinos, Inc. (LACI)
Latin American Casinos, Inc. (LACIW)
Latitude Communications, Inc. (LATD)
Lattice Semiconductor (LSCC)
Launch Media, Inc. (LAUN)
Laurel Capital Group, Inc. (LARL)
Lawrence Savings Bank (LSBX)
Leadville Corporation (LEAD)
Learning Tree International (LTRE)
LEC Technologies, Inc. (LECEP)
Leeds Federal Savings Bank (LFED)
Legacy Software, Inc. (LGCY)
Leisureways Marketing Ltd. (LMLAF)
Letchworth Independent (LEBC)
Level 3 Communications, Inc. (LVLT)
Lexford Inc. (CRSI)
Lexington B & L Financial (LXMO)
Lexington Global Asset (LGAM)
Lexington Healthcare Group (LEXI)
Lexington Healthcare Group (LEXIW)
LGS Group Inc. (LGSAF)
Liberate Technologies, Inc. (LBRT)
Liberty Bancorp, Inc. (LIBB)
Liberty Homes, Inc. (LIBHB)
Liberty Technologies, Inc. (LIBT)
Life Medical Sciences, Inc. (CHAIZ)
Lifetime Hoan Corporation (LCUT)
Lifeway Foods, Inc. (LWAY)
LightPath Technologies, Inc. (LPTHA)
LightPath Technologies, Inc. (LPTHW)
Lihir Gold, Limited (LIHRY)
Lincare Holdings, Inc. (LNCR)
Lincoln Bancorp (LNCB)
Lindal Cedar Homes, Inc. (LNDL)
Lindberg Corporation (LIND)

COMPANY (SYMBOL)

Lionbridge Technologies, Inc. (LIOX)
Liqui-Box Corporation (LIQB)
Liquid Audio, Inc. (LQID)
Litchfield Financial (LTCH)
Litronic Inc. (LTNX)
Littlefuse, Inc. (LFUSW)
Liuski International, Inc. (LSKI)
LJL Biosystems, Inc. (LJLB)
LM Ericsson Telephone Company (ERICY)
LMI Aerospace, Inc. (LMIA)
Local Financial Corporation (LFIN)
Log On America, Inc. (LOAX)
London Financial Corporation (LONF)
London International Group PLC (LONDY)
London Pacific Group, Limited (LPGLY)
LookSmart, Ltd. (LOOK)
Lowrance Electronics, Inc. (LEIX)
Lucor, Inc. (LUCR)
Lufkin Industries, Inc. (LUFK)
Lukens Medical Corporation (LUKN)
Lycos, Inc. (LCOS)
Lynx Therapeutics, Inc. (LYNX)

M

MACC Private Equities Inc. (MACC)
MacDermid, Incorporated (MACD)
Mackenzie Financial (MKFCF)
Mackie Designs, Inc. (MKIE)
Made2Manage Systems, Inc. (MTMS)
Madison Bancshares Group, Ltd. (MADB)
Magainin Pharmaceuticals Inc. (MAGN)
Mahaska Investment Company (OSKY)
Mahoning National Bancorp (MGNB)
Mail.com, Inc. (MAIL)
Maker Communications, Inc. (MAKR)
Makita Corp. (MKTAY)
Managed Care Solutions, Inc. (MCSX)
Manatron, Inc. (MANA)
Manhattan Associates, Inc. (MANH)
Mannatech, Inc. (MTEX)
Mansur Industries Inc. (MANS)
MapQuest.com, Inc. (MQST)
Marimba, Inc. (MRBA)
Marine Management Systems (MMSY)
Marine Management Systems (MMSYW)
Market Financial Corporation (MRKF)
MarketWatch.com, Inc. (MKTW)

COMPANY (SYMBOL)

Marquette Medical Systems, Inc. (MARQ)
Marsh Supermarkets, Inc. (MARSA)
MAS Technology Limited (MASSY)
Mason-Dixon Bancshares, Inc. (MSDXP)
MASSBANK Corp. (MASB)
Master Graphics, Inc. (MAGR)
Maverick Tube Corporation (MAVK)
Max & Erma's Restaurants, Inc. (MAXE)
Maxco, Inc. (MAXC)
Maxtor Corp. (MXTR)
Maxwell Shoe Company Inc. (MAXS)
Mayflower Co-operative Bank (MFLR)
Maynard Oil Company (MOIL)
Mazel Stores, Inc. (MAZL)
MBLA Financial Corporation (MBLF)
MBV Corp. (MFBC)
McClain Industries, Inc. (MCCL)
McGrath RentCorp (MGRC)
McLeod USA, Inc. (MCLDP)
McLeodUSA Incorporated (MCLD)
MCM Capital Group, Inc. (MCMC)
MDC Communications Corporation (MDCAF)
Meadow Valley Corporation (MVCO)
Meadowbrook Rehabilitation (MBRK)
Mechanical Technology, Inc. (MKTY)
MEDE AMERICA Corp. (MEDE)
Media Metrix, Inc. (MMXI)
Medical Control, Inc. (MDCL)
Medical Graphics Corporation (MGCC)
Mediconsult.com, Inc. (MCNS)
Medwave, Inc. (MDWV)
MEEMIC Holdings, Inc. (MEMH)
MegaBank Financial Corp. (MBFC)
Men's Wearhouse, Inc. (The) (SUITG)
Mercantile Bank Corporation (MBWM)
Merchants Bancshares, Inc. (MBVT)
Merchants New York Bancorp (MBNY)
Mercury Computer Systems (MRCY)
Meridian Insurance Group, Inc. (MIGI)
Meritrust Federal Savings Bank (MERI)
Merkert American Corporation (MERK)
Merrill Merchants Bancshares, Inc. (MERB)
Mes/Waste, Inc. (MWDS)
Methode Electronics, Inc. (METHB)
Metro Global Media, Inc. (MCMA)
Metro Information Services (MISI)
MetroBanCorp (METB)

COMPANY (SYMBOL)

MetroCorp Bancshares, Inc. (MCBI)
Metropolitan Financial Corp. (METF)
Metrotrans Corporation (MTRN)
MFRI, Inc. (MFRI)
MGC Communications, Inc. (MGCX)
Michigan Financial Corporation (MFCB)
Microcide Pharmaceuticals (MCDE)
Microenergy, Inc. (MICRP)
Microfield Graphics, Inc. (MICG)
Microframe, Inc. (MCFR)
Micro-Integration Corp. (MINT)
Micromuse, Inc. (MUSE)
Micron Electronics, Inc. (MUEI)
Micronetics Wireless, Inc. (NOIZ)
Microsoft Corporation (MSFT)
Microsoft Corporation (MSFTP)
Microstrategy, Inc. (MSTR)
Microtest, Inc. (MTST)
Mid Continent Bancshares, Inc. (MCBS)
Mid-Atlantic Community (MABG)
Midatlantic Corp. (PNCCG)
Mid-Coast Bancorp, Inc. (MCBN)
Middle Bay Oil Company, Inc. (MBOC)
Middlesex Water Company (MSEX)
Midland Company (The) (MLAN)
Midway Airlines Corporation (MDWY)
Midwest Bancshares, Inc. (MWBI)
Midwest Bank Holdings, Inc. (MBHI)
Midwest Grain Products, Inc. (MWGP)
MIH Ltd. (MIHL)
Mikron Instrument Company (MIKR)
Milbrook Press, Inc. (The) (MILB)
Miller Building Systems, Inc. (MBSI)
Miller Exploration Company (MEXP)
Milton Federal Financial (MFFC)
Mine Safety Appliances Company
  (MNES)
Mining Services International (MSIX)
MiningCo.com, Inc. (MINE)
Minuteman International Inc. (MMAN)
MIPS Technologies, Inc. (MIPS)
Mission Critical Software, Inc. (MCSW)
Mississippi Valley Bancshares (MVBIP)
Mississippi View Holding (MIVI)
Mitsui & Company, Ltd. (MITSY)
Mity-Life, Inc. (MITY)
MKS Instruments, Inc. (MKSI)
MLC Holdings, Inc. (MLCH)
MNB Bancshares Inc. (MNBB)
Mobile Mini, Inc. (MINIW)

COMPANY (SYMBOL)

Mobile Mini, Inc. (MINIZ)
Mobius Management Systems, Inc.
  (MOBI)
Modern Controls, Inc. (MOCO)
Modern Media Poppe Tyson, Inc.
  (MMPT)
Momentum Business Applications, Inc.
  (MMTM)
Monarch Avalon, Inc. (MAHI)
Monmouth Capital Corporation (MONM)
Moore Products Co. (MORP)
Moore-Handley, Inc. (MHCO)
Mortgage.com, Inc. (MDCM)
Motor Cargo Industries, Inc. (CRGO)
Motor Club of America (MOTR)
Motro Vac Technologies, Inc. (MVAC)
Movado Group Inc. (MOVA)
Moyco Technologies, Inc. (MOYC)
MP3.com, Inc. (MPPP)
Mpath Interactive, Inc. (MPTH)
MPW Industrial Services Group (MPWG)
MSB Financial, Inc. (MSBF)
Multex.com, Inc. (MLTX)
Multi-Color Corporation (LABL)
Multimedia Games, Inc. (MGAMW)
Multimedia Games, Inc. (MGAMZ)
Musicmaker.com, Inc. (HITS)
M-WAVE, Inc. (MWAV)
Mycogen Corporation (MYCO)
MyPoints.com, Inc. (MYPT)
Mystic Financial, Inc. (MYST)

N

N2H2, Inc. (NTWO)
NAM Corporation (NAMC)
NAM Corporation (NAMCU)
NAM Corporation (NAMCW)
Nanoen, Inc. (NGEN)
Napco Security Systems, Inc. (NSSC)
Nara Bank, National Association (NARA)
Nastech Pharmaceutical (NSTK)
National Bancorp of Alaska (NBAK)
National City Bancorporation (NCBM)
National City Bancshares, Inc. (NCBE)
National Datacomputer, Inc. (IDCP)
National Environmental Service (NESC)
National Home Centers, Inc. (NHCI)
National Home Health Care (NHHC)
National Income Realty Trust (NIRTS)
National Information Consortium (EGOV)

COMPANY (SYMBOL)

National Medical Health Card Systems (NMHC)
National Security Group, Inc. (NSEC)
Natrol, Inc. (NTOL)
NAVIDEC, Inc. (NVDC)
Navigant International, Inc. (FLYR)
NEI WebWorld, Inc. (NEIP)
Neo Therapeutics, Inc. (NEOTW)
NEON Systems, Inc. (NESY)
NeoPharm, Inc. (NPRMW)
NeoRx Corporation (NERX)
NeoRx Corporation (NERXP)
NeoRx Corporation (NERXW)
Neose Technologies, Inc. (NTEC)
Nera AS (NERAY)
Net Perceptions, Inc. (NETP)
Net2Phone, Inc. (NTOP)
Net.B@ank, Inc. (NTBK)
NetCom Systems, AB (publ) (NECSY)
NetGravity, Inc. (NETG)
Netia Holdings SA (NTIA)
NetIQ Corporation (NTIQ)
Netivation.com Inc. (NTVN)
NetObjects, Inc. (NETO)
Netro Corporation (NTRO)
NetScout Systems, Inc. (NTCT)
Netter Digital Entertainment (NETT)
Netter Digital Entertainment (NETTW)
Network Access Solutions Corp. (NASC)
Network Computing Devices (NCDI)
Network Connection, Inc. (The) (TNCX)
Network Imaging Corporation (IMGXP)
Network Imaging Corporation (IMGXW)
Network Plus Corp. (NPLS)
Network Six, Inc. (NWSS)
Neutral Posture Ergonomics (NTRL)
NevStar Gaming Corporation (NVSTW)
New Brunswick Scientific Co. (NBSC)
New England Community Bancorp (NECB)
New England Realty Associates (NEWRZ)
New Hampshire Thrift (NHTB)
New Horizon Kids Quest, Inc. (KIDQ)
New York Health Care, Inc. (NYHC)
NewCare Health Corporation (NWCA)
Newgen Results Corporation (NWGN)
Newmark Homes Corporation (NHCH)
NewMil Bancorp, Inc. (NMSB)
NewSouth Bancorp, Inc. (NSBC)

COMPANY (SYMBOL)

NextCard, Inc. (NXCD)
Nextel Communications, Inc. (NXTL)
Nextera Enterprises, Inc. (NXRA)
NextHealth, Inc. (NEXT)
nFront, Inc. (NFNT)
Niagara Bancorp, Inc. (NBCP)
Nicholas Financial, Inc. (NICKF)
Nicollet Process Engineering (NPET)
Nitches, Inc. (NICH)
NMBT CORP (NMBT)
Noble International, Ltd. (NOBLN)
Noland Company (NOLD)
Norstan, Inc. (NRRD)
Nortech Systems Incorporated (NSYS)
North American Palladium Ltd. (PDLCF)
North American Scientific, Inc. (NASI)
North Bancshares, Inc. (NBSI)
North County Bancorp (NCBH)
North Pittsburgh Systems, Inc. (NPSI)
Northeast Indiana Bancorp (NEIB)
NorthEast Optic Network, Inc. (NOPT)
Northern States Financial (NSFC)
NorthPoint Communications Group, Inc. (NPNT)
Northrim Bank (NRIM)
Northway Financial Inc. (NWFI)
Northwest Teleproductions (NWTL)
Norwood Financial Corp. (NWFL)
Norwood Promotional (NPPI)
Notify Corporation (NTFY)
Notify Corporation (NTFYU)
Notify Corporation (NTFYW)
Novadigm, Inc. (NVDM)
NovaMed Eyecare, Inc. (NOVA)
Novamerican Steel, Inc. (TONSF)
Novametrix Medical Systems (NMTXZ)
Novitron International, Inc. (NOVI)
NPC International, Inc. (NPCI)
NRG Generating (U.S.) Inc. (NRGG)
NS&L Bancorp, Inc. (NSLB)
NSD Bancorp, Inc. (NSDB)
NTL Incorporated (NTLI)
NTN Canada, Inc. (NTNC)
Nucentrix Broadband Networks (NCNX)
Nutmeg Federal Savings & Loan (NTMG)
Nutmeg Federal Savings & Loan (NTMGP)
Nutraceutical International Corp. (NUTR)
Nutrition For Life (NFLIW)

COMPANY (SYMBOL)

NuWave Technologies, Inc. (WAVE)
NuWave Technologies, Inc. (WAVEW)
NVIDIA Corp. (NVDA)
N-Viro International (NVIC)

O

Oak Hill Financial, Inc. (OAKF)
Oakhurst Company, Inc. (OAKC)
Obie Media Corporation (OBIE)
ObjectSoft Corporation (OSFT)
ObjectSoft Corporation (OSFTW)
Oce NV (OCENY)
Officeland Inc. (OFLUF)
Ohio Valley Banc Corp. (OVBC)
OHM Corporation (OHMCG)
OHSL Financial Corp. (OHSL)
Oilgear Company (The) (OLGR)
Old Kent Financial Corporation (OKEN)
Old Second Bancorp, Inc. (OSBC)
Olicom A/S (OLCWF)
Olympic Cascade Financial (NATS)
Olympic Steel, Inc. (ZEUS)
OMNI Energy Services Corp. (OMNI)
Omni Insurance Group, Inc. (OMGR)
On Stage Entertainment, Inc. (ONSTW)
OneLink Communication, Inc. (ONEL)
OneMain.com, Inc. (ONEM)
OneSource Information Services (ONES)
Online Resource & Communications
  (ORCC)
Online System Services, Inc. (WEBB)
onlinetradinginc.com (LINE)
On-Site Sourcing, Inc. (ONSSU)
On-Site Sourcing, Inc. (ONSSW)
ONYX Software Corporation (ONXS)
Open Plan Systems, Inc. (PLAN)
Ophthalmic Imaging Systems (OISI)
Optelecom, Inc. (OPTC)
Optibase Ltd. (OBAS)
Optika Imaging Systems, Inc. (OPTK)
Optimax Industries, Inc. (OPMXZ)
OptiSystems Solutions, Ltd. (OPTLF)
OptiSystems Solutions, Ltd. (OPTWF)
Oracle Corporation (ORCL)
Orange National Bancorp (OGNB)
Oregon Trail Financial Corp. (OTFC)
Orlando Predators (The) (PRED)
Orlando Predators (The) (PREDW)
OroAmerica, Inc. (OROA)
Ortec International, Inc. (ORTC)

COMPANY (SYMBOL)

Ortec International, Inc. (ORTCW)
Ortec International, Inc. (ORTCZ)
OrthAlliance, Inc. (ORAL)
Oshkosh Truck Corporation (OTRKB)
OSI Systems, Inc. (OSIS)
Otter Tail Power Company (OTTR)
Outlook Group Corp. (OUTL)
OYO Geospace Corporation (OYOG)
Ozark Capital Trust (OZRKP)

P

P & F Industries, Inc. (PFINA)
P. F. Chang's China Bistro, Inc. (PCFB)
PACE Health Management (PCES)
Pacific Capital Bancorp (PABN)
Pacific Coast Apparel Company (ACAJ)
Pacific Crest Capital, Inc. (PCCI)
Pacific Crest Capital, Inc. (PCCIP)
PacifiCare Health Systems (PHSYB)
Packaged Ice, Inc. (ICED)
Packeteer, Inc. (PKTR)
PalEx, Inc. (PALX)
Palm Harbor Homes, Inc. (PHHM)
Pamrapo Bancorp, Inc. (PBCI)
Pancho's Mexican Buffet, Inc. (PAMX)
Paradigm Geophysical, Ltd. (PGEOF)
Paradigm Medical Industries (PMED)
Paradise, Inc. (PARF)
Paradise Music & Entertainment (PDSE)
Paradise Music & Entertainment
  (PDSEW)
Paradyne Networks, Inc. (PDYN)
Paramark Enterprises, Inc. (TJCWC)
Paramark Enterprises, Inc. (TJCZC)
Paramount Financial (PARAW)
Paris Corporation (PBFI)
Pathfinder Bancorp, Inc. (PBHC)
Patient Infosystems, Inc. (PATI)
Patriot Bank Corp. (PBIX)
Paul Harris Stores, Inc. (PAUH)
Paul Mueller Company (MUEL)
Paulson Capital Corp. (PLCC)
PBOC Holdings, Inc. (PBOC)
PC Connection, Inc. (PCCC)
PC411, Inc. (PCFRU)
PC411, Inc. (PCFRW)
PCA International, Inc. (PCAI)
PCC Group, Inc. (PCCG)
pcOrder.com, Inc. (PCOR)
PDK Labs, Inc. (PDKLP)

COMPANY (SYMBOL)

Peak International Limited (PEAKF)
Pease Oil & Gas Company (WPOGW)
Peekskill Financial (PEEK)
Peerless Manufacturing Company
  (PMFG)
Pegasus Communications (PGTV)
Penn National Gaming, Inc. (PENN)
PennFed Financial Services (PFSBP)
PennFirst Bancorp, Inc. (PWBC)
PennFirst Bancorp, Inc. (PWBCP)
Pennichuck Corporation (PNNW)
Pennsylvania Manufacturers Corp.
  (PMFRA)
Pennwood Bancorp, Inc. (PWBK)
People's Bancshares, Inc. (PBKBP)
Peoples BancTrust Company (PBTC)
Peoples Bank (PEBK)
Peoples Financial Corporation (PFFC)
Peoples First Corporation (PFKY)
Peoples Home Savings Bank (PHSB)
Permanent Bancorp, Inc. (PERM)
Perpetual Midwest Financial (PMFI)
Perry County Financial (PCBC)
PerSeptive Biosystems, Inc. (PBIO)
PerSeptive Biosystems, Inc. (PBIOW)
Persistence Software, Inc. (PRSW)
Pete's Brewing Company (WIKD)
Petro Union, Inc. d/b/a (HVNV)
PetroCorp Incorporated (PETR)
Petroglyph Energy, Inc. (PGEI)
Petroleum Helicopters, Inc. (PHEL)
Petroleum Helicopters, Inc. (PHELK)
Petromet Resources Limited (PNTGF)
Petrominerals Corporation (PTRO)
Phar-Mor, Inc. (PMORW)
PHC, Inc. (PIHCW)
Phoenix International Ltd. (PHXX)
Phoenix International Sciences, Inc.
  (PHXI)
Phone.com, Inc. (PHCM)
Photo Control Corporation (PHOC)
Photoelectron Corporation (PECX)
Photomatrix, Inc. (PHRX)
PhyCor, Inc. (PHYCH)
Physicians Health Services (PHSV)
Physicians' Specialty Corp. (ENTS)
PICO Holdings Inc. (PICO)
PictureTel Corporation (PCTL)
Piemonte Foods, Inc. (PIFI)
Piercing Pagoda, Inc. (PGDA)

COMPANY (SYMBOL)

Pilot Network Services, Inc. (PILT)
Pinnacle Financial Services (PNFI)
Pinnacle Holdings Inc. (BIGT)
Pioneer Commercial Funding (PCFC)
Piranha Interactive Publishing (PRAN)
Pittsburgh Home Capital Trust I (PHFCP)
Pittsburgh Home Financial (PHFC)
Pivotal Corporation (PVTL)
Plasti-Line, Inc. (SIGN)
PLX Technology, Inc. (PLXT)
Polymer Research Corp. of America
  (PROA)
PNB Financial Group (PNBF)
Pocahontas Federal Savings (PFSL)
Point of Sale Limited (POSIF)
Pointe Financial Corporation (PNTE)
PolyMedica Corporation (PLMD)
Pope Resources (POPEZ)
Popular, Inc. (BPOPP)
Portal Software, Inc. (PRSF)
Potters Financial Corporation (PTRS)
Premier Concepts, Inc. (FAUX)
Premier Financial Bancorp (PFBI)
Prestige Bancorp, Inc. (PRBC)
Priceline.com, Inc. (PCLN)
Pride Automotive Group, Inc. (LEAS)
Prima Energy Corporation (PENG)
PrimaCom AG (PCAG)
Prime Bancshares, Inc. (PBTX)
Prime Capital Corporation (PMCP)
PrimeEnergy Corporation (PNRG)
Primus Knowledge Solutions (PKSI)
Princeton National Bancorp (PNBC)
Printware, Inc. (PRTW)
Priority Healthcare (PHCC)
Private Business, Inc. (PBIZ)
Private Media Group, Inc. (PRVT)
PrivateBancorp, Inc. (PVTB)
Prodigy Communications Corp. (PRGY)
Producers Entertainment Group (TPEGP)
Producers Entertainment Group (TPEGW)
Productivity Technologies (PRAC)
Productivity Technologies (PRACW)
Professional Detailing, Inc. (PDII)
Professional Transportation (TRUC)
Professional Transportation (TRUCW)
Profile Technologies, Inc. (PRTK)
Progenitor, Inc. (PGENW)
Progressive Bank, Inc. (PSBK)
Projectavision, Inc. (PJTVP)

COMPANY (SYMBOL)

PROLOGIC Management Systems
   (PRLO)
PROLOGIC Management Systems
   (PRLOW)
ProMedCo Management Company
   (PMCO)
Prophet 21, Inc. (PXXI)
Prosperity Bancshares, Inc. (PRSP)
Protein Polymer Technologies (PPTIW)
Provant, Inc. (POVT)
Provident American Corporation (PAMC)
Provident Bancorp, Incorporated (PBCP)
Province Healthcare Company (PRHC)
Proxicom, Inc. (PXCM)
PS Financial, Inc. (PSFI)
Pulaski Financial Corp. (PULB)
Pulse Bancorp, Inc. (PULS)
Pure World, Inc. (PURW)

Q

QIAGEN N.V. (QGENF)
Quadrax Corporation (QDRXZ)
Quepasa.com, Inc. (PASA)
Quest Medical, Inc. (QMED)
Quest Software, Inc. (USFT)
Questa Oil & Gas Co. (QUES)
QuesTech, Inc. (QTEC)
Quidel Corporation (QDELW)
Quiksilver, Inc. (QUIK)
Quizno's Corporation (QUIZ)
Quokka Sports, Inc. (QKKA)
Quotesmith.com, Inc. (QUOT)
Qwest Communications International, Inc.
   (QWST)

R

R & R, Inc. (RBIN)
Radio One, Inc. (ROIA)
Rag Shops, Inc. (RAGS)
RailWorks Corp. (RWKS)
Rainbow Rentals, Inc. (RBOW)
Ramp Networks, Inc. (RAMP)
Rand Capital Corporation (RAND)
Randgold & Exploration (RANGY)
Rankin Automotive Group, Inc. (RAVE)
Raven Industries, Inc. (RAVN)
Ravenswood Winery, Inc. (RVWD)
RAVISENT Technologies Inc. (RVST)
Rawson-Koenig, Inc. (RAKO)

COMPANY (SYMBOL)

Razorfish, Inc. (RAZF)
RCM Technologies, Inc. (RCMTZ)
Reading Entertainment, Inc. (RDGE)
Real Goods Trading Corporation (RGTC)
Realco, Inc. (RLCO)
Realco, Inc. (RLCOW)
Reality Interactive, Inc. (RINT)
Reality Interactive, Inc. (RINTW)
Realty Information Group, Inc. (RIGX)
Reckson Services Industries, Inc. (RSII)
Reconditioned Systems, Inc. (RESY)
Recovery Network, Inc. (The) (RNETU)
Red Hat, Inc. (RHAT)
Red Hot Concepts, Inc. (RHCDC)
Redback Networks, Inc. (RBAK)
Redwood Empire Bancorp (REBC)
Reeds Jewelers, Inc. (REED)
Regency Bancorp (REFN)
Regeneron Pharmaceuticals (REGN)
Regent Assist Living, Inc. (RGNT)
Regent Bancshares Corp. (RBNK)
Reliv' International, Inc. (RELV)
Remington Oil and Gas (ROILAA)
Renaissance Capital Growth & Income
   Fund III, Inc. (RENN)
Renaissance Entertainment (FAIRW)
Renaissance Entertainment (FAIRZ)
Rent-A-Wreck of America, Inc. (RAWA)
Reptron Electronics, Inc. (REPT)
Republic Bancorp Inc., Class A
   (RBCAA)
Republic Bancshares, Inc. (REPB)
Republic Bancshares, Inc. (REPBP)
Republic Security Financial (RSFCO)
Research in Motion Ltd. (RIMM)
Resource Bank (RBKV)
Restoration Hardware, Inc. (RSTO)
Resurgence Properties, Inc. (RPIA)
Retrospettiva, Inc. (RTRO)
Reunion Industries Inc. (RUNI)
Reuters Holdings PLC ADR (RTRSY)
Revenue Properties Company (RPCLF)
Rexall Sundown, Inc. (REXD)
Rexall Sundown, Inc. (RXSD)
Rexhall Industries, Inc. (REXL)
RF Industries, Inc. (RFIL)
Rhythms NetConnections, Inc. (RTHM)
Richmond County Financial Corp.
   (RCBK)

COMPANY (SYMBOL)

Ridgeview, Inc. (RIDG)
Ridgewood Financial, Incorporated
  (RSBI)
Rimage Corporation (RIMG)
Ringer Corporation (RING)
Risk Capital Holdings, Inc. (RCHI)
Riverview Bancorp Inc. (RVSB)
Riviana Foods Inc. (RVFD)
Roanoke Gas Company (RGCO)
Roberds, Inc. (RBDS)
RockShox, Inc. (RSHX)
Rocky Mountain Chocolate (RMCF)
Rocky Mountain Internet, Inc. (RMIIU)
Romac International, Inc. (ROMC)
Ronson Corporation (RONC)
Room Plus, Inc. (PLUS)
Room Plus, Inc. (PLUSW)
Rose's Holdings Inc. (RSTOW)
Rottlund Company, Inc. (The) (RHOM)
RoweCom Inc. (ROWE)
Roy F. Weston, Inc. (WSTNA)
Royal Gold, Inc. (RGLD)
Royal Olympic Cruise Lines, Inc.
  (ROCLF)
Royal Precision, Inc. (RIFL)
RPM, Inc. (RPOWG)
RSI Systems, Inc. (RSIS)
Rubio's Restaurants, Inc. (RUBO)
Russel Metals, Inc. (RUSAF)
Ryan, Beck & Co., Inc. (RBCO)

S

S & K Famous Brands, Inc. (SKFB)
S I Technologies Inc. (SISI)
S & T Bancorp, Inc. (STBA)
S2 Golf Inc. (GOLF)
SAES Getters S.P.A. (SAESY)
Sage Laboratories, Inc. (SLAB)
Sagebrush, Inc. (SAGE)
Sagent Technology, Inc. (SGNT)
Saint Andrews Golf Corporation (SAGC)
Salem Communications Corp. (SALM)
SalesLogix Corporation (SLGX)
Saliva Diagnostic Systems (SALVW)
Salon.com Inc. (SALN)
Sands Regent (The) (SNDS)
Sandy Spring Bancorp, Inc. (SASR)
Sanmina Corporation (SANM)
Santa Barbara Bancorp (SABB)

COMPANY (SYMBOL)

Santa Fe Financial Corporation (SFEF)
Santos, Ltd. (STOSY)
SanVec Company (1990), Ltd. (SVECF)
Sanyo Electric Co., Ltd. (SANYY)
Sawako Corporation (SWKOY)
SBA Communications Corp. (SBAC)
SCC Communications Corp. (SCCX)
Scherer Healthcare, Inc. (SCHR)
School Specialty, Inc. (SCHS)
Schuler Homes, Inc. (SHLRG)
Schultz Sav-O Stores, Inc. (SAVO)
Scient Corporation (SCNT)
Scientific Learning Corp. (SCIL)
Scientific Technologies (STIZ)
Scottish Annuity & Life Holdings, Ltd.
  (SCTLF)
Seacoast Banking Corporation (SBCFA)
Seacoast Financial Services Corp. (SCFS)
Search Financial Services Inc. (SFSI)
Search Financial Services, Inc. (SFSIP)
Seaway Food Town, Inc. (SEWY)
Second Bancorp, Incorporated (SECD)
Second National Financial Corp. (SEFC)
Security First Corp. (SFSL)
Security National Financial (SNFCA)
Seibels Bruce Group, Inc. (SBIG)
Select Comfort Corporation (AIRB)
SEMCO Energy, Inc. (SMGS)
Seminis, Inc. (SMNS)
Senior Tour Players (SRTR)
Senior Tour Players (SRTRW)
Sento Technical Innovations (SNTO)
SERENA Software, Inc. (SRNA)
Serengeti Eyewear, Inc. (SOLR)
Serengeti Eyewear Inc. (SOLRW)
Sevenson Environmental (SEVN)
SFS Bancorp, Inc. (SFED)
SFX Broadcasting, Inc. (SFXBW)
SGV Bancorp, Inc. (SGVB)
Sheridan Energy, Inc. (SHDN)
Shire Pharmaceuticals Group (SHPY)
Shoe Pavilion, Inc. (SHOE)
Sho-Me Financial Corp. (SMFC)
Shoreline Financial (SLFC)
Showcase Corporation (SHWC)
SI Handling Systems, Inc. (SIHS)
Siebel Systems, Inc. (SEBL)
Siebert Financial Corp. (SIEB)
SigmaTron International, Inc. (SGMA)

COMPANY (SYMBOL)

Signature Inns, Inc. (SNGSP)
Silknet Software, Inc. (SILK)
SilverStream Software, Inc. (SSSW)
Simmons First National (SFNCA)
Simmons First National (SFNCP)
Simulation Sciences, Inc. (SMCI)
Simulations Plus, Inc. (SIMU)
Sinclair Broadcast Group, Inc. (SBGIP)
Six Rivers National Bank (SIXR)
SJNB Financial Corp. (SJNB)
Sky Network Television Limited
   (NZSKY)
SkyePharma PLC (SKYYV)
Skylands Community Bank (SKCB)
Skyline Multimedia (SKYL)
Skyline Multimedia (SKYLU)
Skyline Multimedia (SKYLW)
Smartserv Online, Inc. (SSOLW)
SMED International, Inc. (SMEDF)
Smithfield Companies, Inc. (HAMS)
Smith-Gardner & Associates, Inc. (SGAI)
Smith-Midland Corporation (SMIDW)
SNB Bancshares, Inc. (SNBJ)
Sobieski Bancorp, Inc. (SOBI)
Societe Europeenne de Communication
   S.A. (SECAY)
Societe Europeenne de Communication
   S.A. (SECBY)
SoftNet Systems, Inc. (SOFTN)
Software.com, Inc. (SWCM)
software.net Corporation (SWNT)
SOFTWORKS, Inc. (SWRX)
Sound Advice, Inc. (SUND)
Sound Federal Bancorp (SFFS)
South Alabama Bancorporation (SABC)
South Carolina Community (SCCB)
South Jersey Financial Corporation
   (SJFC)
South Street Financial (SSFC)
Southern Community Bancshares (SCBS)
Southern Missouri Bancorp (SMBC)
Southern Pacific Petroleum N.L. (SPPTY)
Southern Security Life (SSLI)
Southside Bancshares Corp. (SBCO)
Southside Bancshares, Inc. (SBSIP)
Southwest Bancorp, Inc. (OKSBO)
Southwest Bancorp, Inc. (OKSBP)
Southwest Bancshares, Inc. (SWBI)
Southwest Water Company (SWWC)

COMPANY (SYMBOL)

Span-America Medical Systems (SPAN)
Spanlink Communications, Inc. (SPLK)
Sparta Foods, Inc. (SPFO)
Sparta Pharmaceuticals, Inc. (SPTAL)
Sparta Pharmaceuticals, Inc. (SPTAU)
Sparta Pharmaceuticals, Inc. (SPTAW)
Specialized Health Products (SHPI)
Specialty Catalog Corp. (CTLG)
Spec's Music, Inc. (SPEK)
Spectra-Physics Lasers, Inc. (SPLI)
SpectraScience, Inc. (SPSI)
Spectrx, Inc. (SPRX)
Splitrock Services, Inc. (SPLT)
Sport Chalet, Inc. (SPCH)
Sportman's Guide, Inc. (SGDE)
SQL Financials International, Inc. (SQLF)
St. Helena Gold Mines Limited (SGOLY)
Stacey's Buffet, Inc. (SBUFW)
Stake Technology Ltd. (STKLF)
Stamps.com Inc. (STMP)
Stanley Furniture Company (STLY)
Star City Holdings Limited (SCITY)
Star Multi Care Services, Inc. (SMCS)
Star Resources Corporation (SRRCF)
Starcraft Corporation (STCR)
StarMedia Network, Inc. (STRM)
Starmet Corporation (STMT)
State Auto Financial (STFC)
State Financial Services (SFSW)
State of The Art, Inc. (SOTA)
StateFed Financial Corporation (SFFC)
Statis Terminals Group NV (STNV)
Stearns & Lehman, Inc. (SLHN)
Steel Dynamics, Inc. (STLD)
Sterling Bancshares, Inc. (SBIBP)
Sterling Financial Corporation (SLFI)
Sterling Financial Corporation (STSAO)
Sterling West Bancorp (SWBC)
Stet Hellas Telecomm SA (STHLY)
Steven Myers & Associates, Inc. (WINS)
Stirling Cooke Brown Holdings (SCBHF)
Strategic Distribution, Inc. (STRD)
Streamline.com, Inc. (SLNE)
Student Advantage, Inc. (STAD)
STV Group, Inc. (STVI)
Success Bancshares, Inc. (SXNB)
Suffolk Bancorp (SUBK)
Sumitomo Bank of California (SUMI)
Sumitomo Bank of California (SUMIZ)

COMPANY (SYMBOL)

Summit Bancshares, Inc. (SBIT)
Summit Bank Corporation (SBGA)
Summit Financial Corporation (SUMM)
Sun Bancorp, Inc. (SNBC)
Sun Community Bancorp, Ltd. (SCBL)
Sun Hydraulics Corporation (SNHY)
SunPharm Corporation (SUNPU)
Sunshine Mining and Refining (SILVZ)
Super Vision International (SUPVA)
Super Vision International (SUPVZ)
Superior National Insurance (SNTL)
SurModics, Inc. (SRDX)
Surrey, Inc. (SOAPU)
Swedish Match, AB (SWMAY)
Swiss Army Brands Inc. (SABI)
Symbollon Corporation (SYMBA)
Symbollon Corporation (SYMBW)
Symons International Group (SIGC)
Symphonix Devices, Inc. (SMPX)
Synalloy Corporation (SYNC)
Synaptic Pharmaceutical (SNAP)
Synbiotics Corporation (SBIO)
SYNSORB Biotech, Inc. (SYBBF)
Synthetic Industries, Inc. (SIND)
Syscomm International (SYCM)
System Software Associates (SSAXG)
Systems & Computer Technology
   (SCTCG)

T

Take-Two Interactive Software (TTWOW)
Talk City, Inc. (TCTY)
Tandy Brands Accessories, Inc. (TBAC)
Tappan Zee Financial, Inc. (TPNZ)
Taylor Devices, Inc. (TAYD)
TBA Entertainment Corporation
   (TBAEW)
TBC Corporation (TBCC)
TC Pipelines, LP (TCLPZ)
TEAM America Corporation (TMAM)
Team Financial, Inc. (TFIN)
TearDrop Golf Company (TDRPW)
Tech Data Corporation (TECD)
Technisouce, Inc. (TSRC)
TEKELEC (TKLC)
Tekgraf, Inc. (TKGFW)
TeleBanc Financial Corp. (TBFC)
Tele-Communications, Inc. (TCOMP)
Telemundo Group, Inc. (TLMDW)

COMPANY (SYMBOL)

TelePad Corporation (TPADU)
TelePad Corporation (TPADW)
Telesystem International Wireless of
   Canada (TIWIF)
Teletouch Communications, Inc. (TELL)
Teletouch Communications, Inc.
   (TELLW)
Telident, Inc. (TLDT)
Tellabs, Inc. (TLAB)
Tellurian, Inc. (TLRN)
Telscape International, Inc. (TSCPW)
Telular Corporation (WRLS)
Temtex Industries, Inc. (TMTX)
TenFold Corporation (TENF)
Terayon Communication Systems, Inc.
   (TERN)
Tesco Corporation (TESOF)
Tescorp, Inc. (TESCP)
Tetra Tech, Inc. (WATR)
Texoil, Inc. (TXLI)
Texoil, Inc. (TXLIW)
Texoil, Inc. (TXLIZ)
TGC Industries, Inc. (TGCI)
TGC Industries, Inc. (TGCIP)
theglobe.com, Inc. (TGLO)
Thermo-Mizer Environmental (THMZW)
TheStreet.com, Inc. (TSCM)
Thinking Tools, Inc. (TSIM)
Thistle Group Holdings, Co. (THTL)
Thomaston Mills, Inc. (TMSTA)
TIB Financial Corporation (TIBB)
TIBCO Software, Inc. (TIBX)
Ticketmaster Online-CitySearch, Inc.
   (TMCS)
Timber Lodge Steakhouse, Inc. (TBRL)
Timberland Bancorp, Inc. (TSBK)
Time Warner Telecom, Inc. (TWTC)
Titan Pharmaceuticals, Inc. (TTNP)
TLII Liquidating Corporation (TLII)
Top Image Systems, Ltd. (TISWF)
topjobs.net PLC (TJOB)
TOPRO Incorporated (TPROW)
Total Entertainment Restaurant (TENT)
Total-Tel USA Communications (TELU)
Tower Tech, Inc. (TTMT)
Towne Services, Inc. (TWNE)
Tracor, Inc. (TTRRW)
Tractor Supply Company (TSCO)
Trailer Bridge, Inc. (TRBR)

COMPANY (SYMBOL)

Tramford International, Ltd. (TRFDF)
Transaction Systems Architects (TSAI)
TransAmerican Waste Industries (WSTE)
TransCor Waste Services, Inc. (TRCW)
Transgene SA (TRGNY)
Trans-Global Resources N.L. (TGBRY)
Transglobe Energy Corporation (TGLEF)
Trans-Industries, Inc. (TRNI)
Transit Group Inc. (TRGPW)
Transmation, Inc. (TRNS)
Transmedia Asia Pacific, Inc. (MBTA)
Trend Micro, Inc. (TMICV)
Triangle Pacific Corp. (TRIP)
Tri-County Bancorp, Inc. (TRIC)
Trimark Holdings, Inc. (TMRK)
Trimedyne, Inc. (TMED)
Trinity Biotech PLC (TRIBY)
Trinity Biotech PLC (TRIZF)
Trio-Tech International (TRTC)
Triple S Plastics, Inc. (TSSS)
Troy Financial Corp. (TRYF)
Troy Group, Inc. (TROY)
TSI International Software Ltd. (TSFW)
Tuesday Morning Corporation (TUES)
Tufco Technologies, Inc. (TFCO)
Tumbleweed, Inc. (TWED)
Tumbleweed Software Corporation
   (TMWD)
Tut Systems, Inc. (TUTS)
T.V.G. Technologies Ltd. (TVGLF)
T.V.G. Technologies Ltd. (TVGWF)
T.V.G. Technologies Ltd. (TVGZF)
Tweeter Home Entertainment Group, Inc.
   (TWTR)

U

UBICS, Inc. (UBIX)
uBid, Inc. (UBID)
UFP Technologies, Inc. (UFPT)
Ultimate Software Group, Inc. (The)
   (ULTI)
Ultradata Systems (ULTR)
Uncle B's Bakery, Inc. (UNCB)
UNIDYNE Corporation (UDYN)
UNIFAB International, Inc. (UFAB)
UniHolding Corp. (UHLD)
Union Bankshares Corporation (UBSH)
Union Bankshares Capital Trust I
   (UBSCP)

COMPANY (SYMBOL)

Union Community Bancorp (UCBC)
Union Community Bank (UCBC)
UnionBancorp, Inc. (UBCD)
Uniphase Corporation (UNPH)
Unique Casual Restaurants, Inc. (UNIQ)
Uniservice Corp. (UNSRW)
Uniservice Corp. (USNRA)
United Bancorp, Inc. (UBCP)
United Community Financial (UCFC)
United Financial Corp. (UBMT)
United Investors Realty Trust (UIRT)
United News & Media, p.l.c. (UNEWY)
United PanAm Financial Corporation
   (UPFC)
United Pan-Europe Communications NV
   (UPCOY)
United Road Services, Inc. (URSI)
United Security Bancorporation (USBN)
United Television, Inc. (UTVI)
United Therapeutics Corp. (UTHR)
Unity Bancorp, Inc. (UNTY)
Universal American Financial (UHCO)
Universal American Financial (UHCOW)
Universal Automotive (UVSL)
Universal Display Corporation (PANL)
Universal Hospital Services (UHOS)
Universal Mfg. Co. (UFMG)
Universal Stainless & Alloy (USAP)
Ursus Telecom Corporation (UTCC)
US LEC Corp. (CLEC)
US SEARCH.com Inc. (SRCH)
U.S. Bancorp (FBSWW)
U.S. Concrete, Inc. (RMIX)
U.S. Energy Corp. (USEG)
U.S. Energy Systems, Inc. (USEY)
U.S. Home & Garden, Inc. (USHGW)
U.S. Interactive, Inc. (USIT)
U.S. Physical Therapy, Inc. (USPH)
U.S. Plastic Lumber Co. (USPL)
U.S. Transportation Systems (USTSW)
U.S. Vision, Inc. (USVI)
U.S. Xpress Enterprises, Inc. (XPRSA)
U.S.-China Industrial (CHDXW)
USA Networks, Inc. (USAI)
USA Truck, Inc. (USAK)
USANA, Inc. (USNA)
USBANCORP, Inc. (UBAN)
USDATA Corporation (USDC)
USFreightways Corporation (USFC)

COMPANY (SYMBOL)

Usinternetworking, Inc. (USIX)
USN Communications, Inc. (USNC)
USP Real Estate Investment (USPTS)

V

V.I. Technologies, Inc. (VITX)
Vail Banks, Inc. (VAIL)
Valle de Oro Bank NA (VADO)
Vallen Corporation (VALN)
Valley Independent Bank (VAIB)
Valley Media, Inc. (VMIX)
Value America, Inc. (VUSA)
Value Line, Inc. (VALU)
Varian Inc. (VARIV)
VaxGen, Inc. (VXGN)
Vectra Banking Corporation (VTRAO)
Velcro Industries N.V. (VELCF)
Venturian Corp. (VENT)
Verisign, Inc. (VRSN)
VERITAS Software Corporation (VRTS)
Versatel Telecom International (VRSA)
Versatility Inc. (VERS)
VerticaNet, Inc. (VERT)
VIALOG Corp. (VLOG)
Viant Corporation (VIAN)
ViaSat, Inc. (VSAT)
Video Display Corporation (VIDE)
Video Services Corporation (VSCX)
Videonics, Inc. (VDNX)
View Tech, Inc. (VUTKW)
Vignette Corporation (VIGN)
Vinings Investment Properties (VIPIS)
Vion Pharmaceuticals, Inc. (VIONU)
Vion Pharmaceuticals, Inc. (VIONW)
Virginia Capital Bancshares, Inc. (VCAP)
Virginia Commerce Bank (VCBK)
Virginia Gas Company (VGCO)
Virginia Gas Company (VGCOW)
Visual Data Corporation (VDAT)
Visual Networks, Inc. (VNWK)
VISX, Incorporated (VISX)
Vitesse Semiconductor Corporation
   (VTSS)
Vitran Corporation, Inc. (VTNAF)
Voice It Worldwide, Inc. (MEMO)
VoiceStream Wireless Corporation
   (VSTR)
Volvo (A B) (VOLVY)
V-ONE Corporation (VONE)

COMPANY (SYMBOL)

VOXEL (VOXLU)
Voyager.net, Inc. (VOYN)
VRB Bancorp (VRBA)
Vyrex Corporation (VYRXW)
Vysis, Inc. (VYSI)

W

Wall Street Deli, Inc. (WSDI)
Walnut Financial Services (WNUT)
Walsh International, Inc. (WSHI)
Walshire Assurance Company (WALS)
Wandel & Goltermann (WGTI)
Warner Chilcott Public Limited
   (WCRXY)
Warrantech Corporation (WTEC)
Warren Bancorp, Inc. (WRNB)
Warwick Community Bancorp, Inc.
   (WSBI)
Warwick Valley Telephone Company
   (WWVY)
Washington Banking Company (WBCO)
Washington Federal, Inc. (WFSL)
Washington Mutual, Inc. (WAMU)
Washington Mutual, Inc. (WAMUM)
Washington Scientific (WSCI)
Waste Connections, Inc. (WCNX)
Waste Industries, Inc. (WWIN)
Waste Systems International (WSII)
WasteMasters, Inc. (WAST)
Waterford Wedgewood PLC (WATFZ)
Water-Jel Technologies Inc. (XCED)
Waters Instruments, Inc. (WTRS)
Watson General Corporation (WGEN)
Wausau-Mosinee Paper (WSAU)
Wave Systems Corp. (WAVX)
Wave Technologies (WAVT)
Wavecom SA (WVCM)
WavePhore, Inc. (WAVO)
Waverly, Inc. (WAVR)
Wayne Bancorp, Inc. (WNNB)
Wayne Bancorp, Inc. (WYNE)
Wayne Savings Bancshares Inc. (WAYN)
WD-40 Company (WDFC)
Webster City Federal Savings (WCFB)
Webster Financial Corporation (WBST)
WebTrends Corporation (WEBT)
Wegener Corporation (WGNR)
WellCare Management Group (The)
   (WELL)

COMPANY (SYMBOL)

Wellington Properties Trust (WLPT)
Werner Enterprises, Inc. (WERN)
WesBanco, Inc. (WSBC)
Wescast Industries, Inc. (WCSTF)
Wesley Jessen VisionCare, Inc. (WJCO)
West Coast Bancorp (WCBO)
West Coast Entertainment Corp. (WCEC)
West Essex Bancorp, Inc. (WEBK)
West Marine, Inc. (WMAR)
West TeleServices Corporation (WTSC)
WestAmerica Corporation (WACC)
WestBank Corporation (WBKC)
Westell Technologies, Inc. (WSTL)
Westerbeke Corporation (WTBK)
WesterFed Financial (WSTR)
Western Bancorp (WEBC)
Western Bancorp (WEFC)
Western Beef, Inc. (BEEF)
Western Country Clubs, Inc. (WCCI)
Western Deep Levels Ltd. (WDEPY)
Western Ohio Financial (WOFC)
Western Power & Equipment (WPEC)
Western Sierra Bancorp (WSBA)
Western Staff Services, Inc. (WSTF)
Western Water Company (WWTR)
Western Wireless Corporation (WWCA)
Westernbank Puerto Rico (WBPR)
Westmark Group Holdings, Inc. (WGHI)
WestPoint Stevens Inc. (WPSN)
Westwood Homestead Financial (WEHO)
Westwood One, Inc. (WONE)
Wet Seal, Inc. (The) (WTSLA)
Weyco Group, Inc. (WEYS)
WFS Financial, Inc. (WFSI)
Wheels Sports Group, Inc. (WHEL)
Wheels Sports Group, Inc. (WHELW)
WHG Bancshares Corporation (WHGB)
White Cap Industries, Inc. (WHCP)
White Pine Software, Inc. (WPNE)
White River Corporation (WHRC)
Whitney Holding Corporation (WTNY)
Whittman-Hart, Inc. (WHIT)
Whole Foods Market, Inc. (WFMI)
Wickes Inc. (WIKS)
WideCom Group, Inc. (The) (WIDEF)
WideCom Group, Inc. (The) (WIDWF)
Williamette Valley Vineyards (WVVI)
Williams Controls, Inc. (WMCO)
Williams Industries, Inc. (WMSI)
Williams-Sonoma, Inc. (WSGC)

COMPANY (SYMBOL)

Willis Lease Finance (WLFC)
Willow Grove Bancorp, Inc. (WGBC)
Wilmar Industries, Inc. (WLMR)
Wilshire Real Estate Investment Trust, Inc. (WREI)
Wilshire State Bank (WSBK)
Wilsons The Leather Experts (WLSN)
Wilsons The Leather Experts (WLSNW)
Wind River Systems, Inc. (WIND)
Winfield Capital Corp. (WCAP)
Wink Communications, Inc. (WINK)
Winland Electronics, Inc. (WLET)
WinStar Communications, Inc. (WCII)
Wintrust Capital Trust I (WTFCP)
Wintrust Financial Corporation (WTFC)
Wireless One, Inc. (WIRL)
Wit Capital Group, Inc. (WITC)
Wiztec Solutions, Limited (WIZTF)
WLR Foods, Inc. (WLRF)
WMF Group, Ltd. (The) (WMFG)
Wolohan Lumber Company (WLHN)
Women First Healthcare (WFHC)
Wonderware Corporation (WNDR)
Woodhead Industries, Inc. (WDHD)
Woodroast Systems, Inc. (WRSI)
Woodward Governor Company (WGOV)
Workgroup Technology (WKGP)
World Acceptance Corporation (WRLD)
World Access, Inc. (WAXS)
World Airways, Inc. (WLDA)
World Heart Corporation (WHRTF)
World of Science, Inc. (WOSI)
WorldCom, Inc. (WCOM)
WorldCom, Inc. (WCOMP)
WorldGate Communications, Inc. (WGAT)
Worldtalk Communications (WTLK)
Worthington Foods, Inc. (WFDS)
Worthington Industries, Inc. (WTHG)
WPI Group, Inc. (WPIC)
WPP Group PLC (WPPGY)
WSFS Financial Corporation (WSFS)
WSMP, Inc. (WSMP)
WTD Industries, Inc. (WTDI)
Wyant Corporation (WYNT)
Wyman-Gordon Company (WYMN)

X

XATA Corporation (XATA)
Xeikon, N.V. (XEIKY)

COMPANY (SYMBOL)

Xenometrix, Inc. (XENOW)
Xenova Group PLC (XNVAY)
Xeta Corporation (XETA)
XETel Corporation (XTEL)
XIOX (XICO)
Xircom, Inc. (XIRC)
XLConnect Solutions, Inc. (XLCT)
XOMA Corporation (XOMA)
Xomed Surgical Products, Inc. (XOMD)
Xoom.com, Inc. (XMCM)
XOX Corporation (XOXC)
XOX Corporation (XOXCW)
Xpedite Systems, Inc. (XPED)
X-Rite, Incorporated (XRIT)
XXsys Technologies, Inc. (XSYS)
Xybernaut Corporation (XYBR)

Y

Yahoo! Inc. (YHOO)
Yellow Corporation (YELL)
YES! Entertainment Corporation (YESS)
YieldUP International (YILD)
YieldUp International (YILDZ)
York Financial Group (YFED)

COMPANY (SYMBOL)

York Group, Inc. (The) (YRKG)
York Research Corporation (YORK)
Youbet.com, Inc. (UBET)
Young Broadcasting, Inc. (YBTVA)
Yurie Systems, Inc. (YURI)

Z

Zany Brainy, Inc. (ZANY)
Zebra Technologies Corporation (ZBRA)
Zegarelli Group International, (ZEGG)
ZEVEX International, Inc. (ZVXI)
Zi Corporation (ZICAF)
Zila, Inc. (ZILA)
Zindart Limited (ZNDTY)
Zions Bancorporation (ZION)
ZipLink, Inc. (ZIPL)
Zitel Corporation (ZITL)
Zoll Medical Corporation (ZOLL)
Zomax Optical Media, Inc. (ZOMX)
Zonagen, Inc. (ZONA)
Zoom Telephonics, Inc. (ZOOM)
Zoran Corporation (ZRAN)
Z-Seven Fund, Inc. (ZSEV)
Zygo Corporation (ZIGO)
ZYMETX, Inc. (ZMTX)

BIBLIOGRAPHY

Aspatore, Jonathan. *Fire Your Broker and Trade Online.* New York: McGraw-Hill, 2000.

Baird, Bob, and Craig McBurney. *Electronic Day Trading to Win.* New York: Wiley, 2000.

Farrell, Christopher. *Day Trade Online.* New York: Wiley, 2000.

Friedfertig, Marc, and George West. *The Electronic Day Trader.* New York: McGraw-Hill, 1998.

Gonzales, Fernando, and William Rhee. *Strategies for the Online Day Trader.* New York: McGraw-Hill, 1999.

Harris, Sunny. *Electronic Day Trading 101.* New York: Wiley, 2000.

Nassar, David. *How to Get Started in Electronic Day Trading.* New York: McGraw-Hill, 1999.

Smith, Gary. *How I Trade for a Living.* New York: Wiley, 2000.

INDEX

ABOUT THE AUTHOR

Alicia Abell is the editor for a financial Web site. Formerly an associate editor at *Washingtonian* magazine, she has contributed to numerous books on electronic trading and the Internet, including *The New Electronic Traders*.